The Smart Spending Guide

*How to Cut Your Grocery Bills in Half,
Save on Your Everyday Expenses,
and Live Within Your Means*

Faye Prosser

Magnolia Way Publishing

The Smart Spending Guide

Published by Magnolia Way Publishing
P.O. Box 1688
Clayton, NC 27520

Printed in the United States of America

Library of Congress Control Number: 2005933488

ISBN: 0-9773436-4-2

Dedication

This book is dedicated to my wonderful daughters, Hannah and Emma.

I love you with all my heart.

Acknowledgements

I would like to thank all the talented people who helped bring this book to life including my wonderful editor, Sherri Allen, and very gifted graphic designer, Cathi Stevenson. I also extend my deep gratitude to the skilled peer reviewers who offered immensely valuable feedback, including Kim Cottle, Anjie Hresan-Henley, Marc Katzin, Marian Katzin, Jason Prosser, Carole Rhodes and Rachael Woodard. I will forever appreciate the precious gifts of your time and insight.

A special thank you goes out to my husband, Jason, for his patience, advice, support, and love.

Finally, my heartfelt thanks go out to my parents, Marian and David Katzin, for their endless love, support, and encouragement.

Contents

Introduction

Can you say "YES" to *all* of the following statements?

- ❖ My car is paid off.
- ❖ My mortgage is paid off.
- ❖ I have no credit card debt.
- ❖ I save at least 40% off my grocery bill each month.
- ❖ I have enough money for a comfortable retirement at a reasonable age.
- ❖ I have saved enough to cover six months of expenses if my income drops.
- ❖ I am 100% debt-free and living comfortably within my means.

If your answer to any of the previous statements is "NO," the techniques in this book can make a positive difference in your life. You may be struggling to pay your bills due to job loss, living paycheck to paycheck, wondering where you will get the money to pay for your child's college expenses, concerned that you will not have enough savings to retire, or just looking for a way to keep more of the money that you make. Regardless of your reasons, you owe it to yourself and your family to get and keep your spending under control.

This book is meant to teach you how to make wise choices that will enable you to live comfortably within your means, which is what frugal living is all about. You will learn how to set financial goals, reduce debt, and create and use a budget. In addition, you will discover how to save a significant amount of money on your everyday expenses including groceries, non-food essentials, gifts, telephone service, travel, utilities, prescriptions, entertainment, dining, cleaning supplies and more. And if that weren't enough, you will even find helpful information about how to receive free product samples and earn extra money through surveys and mystery shopping.

Please keep in mind that living within your means does not require you to give up fun for the rest of your life! On the contrary, knowing that you are being a good steward of your hard-earned money will allow you to enjoy your life that much more. The knowledge that you can pay your bills on time every month or that you will be able to enjoy retirement can make everything seem more fulfilling. Plus, there are lots of great ideas for having fun the frugal way in the pages ahead.

The goal of living within your means is one that everyone can reach with a little patience, a good dose of discipline, and the willingness to be flexible. When you combine these traits with the right techniques, you have the winning combination for moving toward a debt-free life.

Keep in mind that this is not a radical frugal living book full of highly unusual and bizarre ways to live on $10 a week. For the record, I do not forage for edible plants along the highway or recycle dryer lint. I do recycle dryer sheets, though; they make fantastic dusting cloths!

This book is written with the beginning to intermediate smart spenders in mind. The Smart Spending Grocery System is an ideal resource for everyone from those who have never used a coupon or frugal living technique in their lives to those who use them but don't see at least 40% savings on their grocery bills each week. This guide is full of tried and true frugal living tips that will help anyone wanting to cut their expenses: college students, newlyweds, parents, retirees, and anyone who eats food, uses water and electricity and makes phone calls!

Remember that you will see the greatest savings by using a combination of many of the techniques, not just one or two.

Some of these methods, such as the Smart Spending Grocery System, will save you large amounts of money. Some will save you smaller amounts and not seem as significant at first. Over time and used in conjunction with the other frugal living and smart spending ideas, even the small savings can add up to big numbers. The key is to use as many of the ideas in this book as possible to stretch your hard-earned dollars all the way to a comfortable retirement.

Where to Start
As you read through the table of contents, you will see that the book is divided into eight different chapters, all of which contain various ways to help you manage your funds and spend less money. I recommend that you read Chapter 1 first, before you dive into the other chapters. Chapter 1 discusses the extremely important subjects of financial goal setting, budgeting and debt reduction. In order to know how much you have to spend on groceries, entertainment, gifts, and all your other expenses each month, you will need to do a realistic and workable budget. Chapter 1 shows you how to do just that. Once you have read through and completed the suggested activities for Chapter 1, you can easily go to any other chapter at any time. The techniques in Chapters 2 through 8 can be read in any order and each chapter makes for a great reference when you need ideas about a particular subject.

The information contained in this book comes from my many years of experience using the recommended techniques and from various frugal living resources. Those resources include, among many wonderful and creative people, my dear, late father-in-law, whose love of frugal living made us kindred souls from the first time we compared grocery store receipts! Where needed, I have included references for resources that offer more detailed information on a subject, including those mentioned in the Resource Directory.

As you jump in to Chapter 1, remember that these are essential first steps to becoming debt-free. If you take these steps seriously, you can have a clear picture of your financial situation and a guide to help you climb the mountain toward financial freedom.

Chapter 1

Financial Reality
Getting Your Financial House in Order

The financial freedom that comes with frugal living and smart spending is founded in solid financial habits. These habits are honed through establishing goals, budgeting and good old-fashioned discipline.

The Path to Financial Clarity
Achieving an accurate picture of your financial situation involves three important steps. These steps are setting financial goals, determining your debt burden and creating a workable budget. As you roll your eyes at the mention of a budget, remember that knowing how much money you have available for specific expenses will take the guesswork out of spending and make it 100% easier to stay on track with your financial goals. Without a budget, you have no clear understanding of where your money is going and no way to ensure that you are on track to meet your important financial milestones.

In your noble endeavor to climb to the heights of financial freedom, there is a clear path you must take. The budget is your guide on this climb. A realistic budget will steer you through the foothills of financial goal setting, taking you slowly up the mountain of debt reduction to the great pinnacle of debt-free living. It will guide you toward the frugal and responsible path when temptation appears. Think of your budget as a friend who only has your best financial interest at heart.

You will need to revisit your budget frequently to make sure you are staying on track. As your debt is reduced and your savings increased, you will be even more motivated to follow your friend's clear spending guidelines and stay within that all important budget. With every new financial height you reach, you will see how truly wonderful goal setting, debt reduction and budgeting can be for you and your family!

Credit Worthiness

As you begin to assess your financial situation, it is important that you review your credit report. This report contains the details of your credit payment history and current credit status. If you apply for a credit card, mortgage, auto loan, apartment lease, student loan, or other type of credit, the lender will almost certainly check your credit report and credit score.

The Fair Isaac Corporation developed the credit score, known as the FICO score. This score is derived from past credit experiences and current debt load using a complex credit-scoring model. The resulting three-digit number, which ranges from 300 to 850, indicates a person's credit risk. The best FICO score is 850 and those with the highest scores will obtain the best interest rates on their credit. Based on your FICO score, a potential creditor will determine whether or not to offer you credit. If your score is high, you will probably be considered a good risk and will likely be extended credit at a reasonable interest rate. If your score is low, you may be denied credit or offered credit with a very high interest rate.

An important part of getting your financial house in order is to check your credit report and make sure that you have "good" credit. If your credit is not acceptable, you must take the necessary steps to improve your credit score. You may be surprised to find your credit report contains errors that are bringing your credit score down, such as debts that you do not owe. In that case, contacting the credit bureaus and correcting the errors will result in a higher credit score.

There is another significant reason for checking your credit report—fraud. In the last few years, there has been a substantial increase in identity theft. If a person uses your name and other identifying information to obtain credit, he or she is influencing your credit score. If you check your credit score regularly (at least once a year) you can identify any fraudulent activity and work with the three national credit bureaus to repair your credit report.

Request Your Free Credit Report

Online:	https://www.annualcreditreport.com
Phone:	877-322-8228
Mail:	Annual Credit Report Request Service
	P.O. Box 105281
	Atlanta, GA 30348-5281

The great news is that a new federal law, issued under the Fair and Accurate Credit Transactions Act, allows you to request a free credit report every 12 months. As of September 1, 2005 people living in the Unites States can request one free yearly credit report from each of the three national credit reporting companies: Equifax, Experian, and TransUnion. You may request your reports by contacting the centralized agency that is run by the three companies either online, by phone or by mail. If you request your report by mail, you will need to fill out the form found on the Annual Credit Report agency Web site at https://www.annualcreditreport.com.

You may request the three credit reports from each of the companies at once or stagger your requests throughout the year.

The free credit report does not include your FICO credit score. You can order your FICO score through the Annual Credit Report website for a fee (currently $6.95). You can also pay to obtain your credit report and FICO score, as well as detailed information on how to improve your score, at http://www.myfico.com.

Keep in mind that you may have a different FICO score for each of the three credit reporting companies. That is because each company may have different information about your credit history and current credit status, which is another excellent reason to check your credit report with each company and correct any errors as soon as possible.

Visit http://www.bankrate.com/brm/news/pf/20001127a.asp for more information on checking your credit report.

Setting Financial Goals

As you begin your quest for financial clarity, you will first need to establish your short-term, medium-term and long-term financial goals. Are you saving for your child's college expenses, for the purchase of a new car, or for ample retirement funds? Would you like to pay off your mortgage in the next 10 years? Do you want to be debt-free within 2 years? Each person's financial goals are different and at this point you need to determine what goals are important for you and your family.

Put your goals in writing: Using the following worksheet, list your *specific and measurable* short-term financial goals (up to 3 years), medium-term financial goals

(3-10 years) and your long-term financial goals (10+ years). Use this list as a motivational tool to keep you headed toward the debt-free mountaintop.

Set a timeframe: You will need to choose a reasonable deadline for reaching your goals. For a helpful online tool, go to http://www.bankrate.com and click on "Calculators." Use the various calculators to determine how much money you will need to save per month to reach each financial goal.

Develop a strategy: Your strategy for attaining your goals needs to be realistic and attainable. You should challenge yourself, but make sure you can actually achieve the goals. Setting the goal to become the richest person in the country in one year might not be realistic and attainable, although, you never know!

Pat yourself on the back: As you reach each goal, check it off to remind yourself how responsible you have been. Celebrate with little incentives, like a picnic in the park or a movie rental with a big bowl of popcorn.

Keep your goals current: As you attain your goals, and as they change, add new goals and amend the list.

Include the kids: Ask for your children's input in goal setting as a way to motivate them to support the goal when they are not able to spend money they would like to spend. You can remind them that you do not have extra money for a trip to the arcade because your family agreed to save for a trip to an exciting amusement park or beach resort the next summer.

Anticipate obstacles: Things will not always go as planned and there will be unexpected issues that get in your way. If you are flexible and have alternate options, you will be more successful in achieving your goals. If things don't happen as you would like them to, redefine the goal or action plan. For instance, you may set the goal of paying off your debt in one year. The obstacle you might face is that you do not earn enough money to make the extra payments required to put toward your debt-reduction goal. You will have to consider alternate options to earn that extra money, including a second job or selling some possessions.

The keys to achieving your financial goals are motivation, commitment and discipline. Start now and don't ever, ever give up! Seek support from your family and friends. Constant reinforcement and encouragement are important for your success. Share your vision for the future, remain positive, and welcome the cheerleading your family and friends can offer! They want to see you succeed as well! Use the following worksheet as a guide while developing your personal financial goals:

Financial Goals Worksheet

Goal	Dollar Amount Needed	Month & Year Needed	# of Months to Save	Savings Start Date	Monthly Savings Amount
Short-Term (up to 3 yrs):					
Med.-Term (3-10 years):					
Long-Term (10+ years):					

Once you have identified your financial goals, you will need to evaluate your debt burden and set up a budget. Remember that your budget is the key to reaching the top of the debt-free mountain.

Getting Out of Debt

In order to experience financial peace of mind, you need to be free of debt. Although many people do not have their houses paid in full, they can work aggressively toward eliminating all other debt, as well as pay off their homes. According to www.myfico.com, a division of Fair Isaac, approximately 10% of credit card holders carry a balance of over $10,000! Using a www.bankrate.com credit card calculator, you will see that if you pay $200 per month, on a $10,000 credit card balance with a 15% Annual Percentage Rate (APR), it will take you over 6.5 years to pay off the debt. Not only will it take you 6.5 years to pay off the credit card, but you will have paid over $5,700 in additional interest during that time. The real cost that you end up paying for that $10,000 debt is $15,700. Do you really want to still be paying for your new home theater system or fancy dinners 6.5 years after the original purchases? I bet your answer is a very clear "NO!"

Those of you who are living beyond your means must make paying off your debt the number one priority. There is just no way to sugarcoat that message. Set a strict, yet workable, budget and stick to it until the debt is paid. You will need to be realistic and disciplined if you intend to dig out from under the debt burden. Sometimes the digging out can take years of serious frugal living. Yet, imagine the incredible freedom you will feel once that debt is paid. Remember, you must be willing to defer having some things you want now to achieve your financial goals.

My husband and I lived in a small home on a busy street for six years in order to pay off car and student loans and save for a down payment on a larger house. I did not love where we were living, but we wanted to pay off the debt before we purchased a larger home and had children. It was not easy to be patient, but if we had we spent the money on a larger house before the debt was paid, we would still have that debt burden today. When we finally purchased a home, we decided not to buy a house that was as big as the bank said we could buy. We bought a house we will stay in for a long time and one we will be able to pay off in a 15-year period. The thought of having our house paid for by the time our children are in high school is just amazing! And it was certainly worth six years of living in a smaller home.

Tips to Remember When Eliminating Debt

- DO NOT continue to incur more debt. Cut up your credit cards and do whatever it takes to keep you from using them to spend more money that you do not have.

- Stick to a budget that involves paying off the credit card or loan with the highest interest rate first, then work your way down until all the debt is gone.

- Ask for help if you need it. Contact your creditors, explain your situation and tell them you want to pay off all your debt in a timely manner. Make sure you ask for a lower interest rate. Often, they will oblige.

- Call a non-profit credit-counseling agency that does not have a vested interest in making money off of your debt. A good resource to start with if you need credit counseling is the National Foundation for Credit Counseling (NFCC) at http://www.nfcc.org and toll free at 1-800-388-2227. The NFCC is a well-known non-profit agency that helps individuals with budgeting and debt reduction plans. Many of their services are free or cost only a minimal fee.

Debt-to-Income Ratio

The debt-to-income ratio is an effective way to compare your debt burden to your total income. It is also one of the leading indicators of financial health used by lenders to determine creditworthiness. To calculate your debt-to-income ratio, add all your minimum monthly debt payments and divide the total by your net (after-tax) monthly income. The monthly minimum debt payments include mortgage, rent, credit card bills, car payments, student loans, child support payments and any other loans you may have. Do not include food, entertainment and utility bills when calculating your debt-to-income ratio.

Debt-to-Income Calculation:

_____ ÷ _____ = _____

| Minimum Monthly | ÷ Net Monthly Income | = Debt-to-Income |
| Debt Payments | | Ratio |

A debt-to-income ratio of .36 (36%) or less generally indicates stronger fiscal health. A ratio of over .36 is cause for concern and must be lowered through debt reduction. When your debt-to-income ratio is high, an unexpected debt, such as a medical bill, could mean financial disaster for your family.

Next, complete the following Debt Payment Worksheet in order to track your debt and clearly see which balances need to be paid first, second, third, etc. To determine how long it will take you to pay off a debt by making a certain payment amount, go to a financial Web site such as http://www.bankrate.com and use the payment calculators. If you are only making minimum payments, you will probably be shocked to see how long it will actually take to pay off your debt.

Debt Payment Worksheet				
Debt (list from highest to lowest interest rate	Balance of Debt	Annual Interest Rate	Minimum Monthly Payment	Payoff Date in Months
1.				
2.				
3.				
4.				
Total Amount of Debt and Payments				

Developing a Budget

Once you have a handle on how much debt you have, it is time to create a formal budget. Developing a budget is not a responsibility to be taken lightly. Remember that a realistic and workable budget is your guide up the financial mountain and will be there to take you to the pinnacle of financial freedom. This is one powerful tool—use it wisely!

Be prepared to sit down with your financial records, a pencil, a calculator, some scrap paper and plenty of chocolate (optional) for at least a couple of hours. Feel free to work on part of the budget one night and finish the next night. It doesn't have to be completed in one marathon session, but don't string your budget planning out too long or you may lose interest and enthusiasm.

To develop your household budget, use the Basic Budget Worksheet found in the Appendix and follow the steps listed below:

1. Look over the worksheet categories and amend them to fit your income and expenses. Add and delete categories as they apply to your specific earnings and spending habits.

2. Calculate your average monthly income including net employment income, spouse's income and all other sources of income.

3. Gather your checkbook, bills and receipts for the last two to three months and average how much you are actually spending per month on the budget categories listed. If you do not have all the information, make your best estimate. You will have the opportunity to discover how much you are really spending later in the chapter.

4. For expenses that occur more or less often than monthly, convert the annual amount to a monthly figure when calculating the monthly budget amount. For instance, if your homeowner's insurance is paid yearly, divide that annual cost by 12 to obtain the monthly amount.

5. Total the income category and total the expenses category.

6. Subtract the total expenses from the total income to calculate your net income.

7. **If your net income is a positive number**, good for you! This means that you have money left over at the end of the month after your expenses have been paid. Apply any extra money to paying off debt and increasing your savings. Remember that extra money left in a checking account tends to be spent.

8. **If your net income is a negative number**, then your expenses equal more than your income and it is time to make some immediate adjustments in your spending. You are living beyond your means and it is time to apply some frugal living techniques right away. Read on to learn the information that will help you reach a positive net income.

9. Update your budget quarterly to see if any changes need to be made and to ensure that you are staying on track. Your budget will be a faithful guide no matter what your financial situation and the key is to continue to live within your means throughout your journey. Your budget will let you know right away if you are spending more than you should. "Listen" to it carefully and heed its warning if you are spending too much.

10. Once you have completed your budget, it is time to record your daily expenditures in order to determine where you can cut expenses and control total spending.

Daily Expenditure Tracking
You knew this was coming - now is the time to record your daily expenditures for one month. You will need to track EVERY SINGLE PENNY you spend during the month, for EVERY SINGLE PERSON in your household. If you think the task is too much to handle, think again. With a simple tracking sheet and 20 minutes a day (what is 20 minutes when your financial future is at stake?), you can get the TRUE picture of how your family is spending your hard-earned income. Can you guess which trait comes in most handy at this point? You guessed it—DISCIPLINE!

Make sure you track all expenditures, including those paid for with cash, credit cards, debit cards and checks. Use the budget worksheet categories and track the various expenses daily for one month. If you have a software program that allows you to enter the information, you will be able to sort and chart the figures more easily.

Regardless of how you enter the expenditures, make sure you do it. This is important for helping you determine which expenses can be reduced, thus increasing your net income.

Once you have tracked all your daily expenses for one month, take a look at what you have spent in each category. You will probably be quite surprised at how much you and your family have spent on convenience items, such as take-out food, sodas at the gas station, lunches out and various miscellaneous expenditures. Now, use this record to determine which expenditures can be cut out completely, or at least lessened, so that your net income is positive and you are paying off debt, not incurring more liabilities.

You have now made it through the eye-opening world of budgeting and should have a much better idea of where you stand financially. Continue to update these tools, especially as your expenses drop due to your diligent use of the Smart Spending Grocery System.

Key Points To Remember

- Maintaining a good credit report is vital to your financial strength. Federal law now allows you to request a free credit report every 12 months.

- Setting specific, measurable and realistic financial goals is a motivating tool that allows you to see exactly how much money you need to be saving to reach your financial objectives.

- If you are living beyond your means, you must make paying off your debt a priority by sticking to a budget that requires you to aggressively pay off your debt.

- Without a budget, you have no real understanding of where your money is going and no way to ensure that you are on track to meet your important financial milestones.

Key Steps To Take

- Check your credit report at no cost every year at https://www.annualcreditreport.com.

- Correct any errors on your credit report as soon as possible. They may be negatively affecting your credit score.

- Complete the Financial Goals Worksheet using specific, measurable and realistic goals.

- Create a workable and realistic budget so you know how much money you have available to spend.

- Track all of your expenses daily for one month to determine how you are actually spending your money. This will enable you to see where you are spending unnecessarily and where you should cut back.

Chapter 2

The Smart Spending Grocery System

The Smart Spending Grocery System offers proven techniques that will help you cut the cost of your grocery and non-food essentials significantly. You will be surprised how easily you can master the system if you are willing to call on our favorite three traits: flexibility, patience and discipline. Reducing grocery expenses does not mean cutting out all the foods you normally eat, it just means planning and shopping a little differently. Considering what you have at stake—your entire financial future— taking charge of your grocery shopping is a good thing!

According to the latest statistics from the U.S. Census Bureau's Statistical Abstract of the United States, the average consumer's annual food expenditure is $5,375. That is a weekly average of $103.37. In comparison, my family spends an average of $50 on groceries each week. Using the Smart Spending Grocery System, my family of four spends less than half of what is spent by the average American family. The funny thing is that we eat better now than we did before we started using the techniques in the system!

Although I spend $50 or less per week, I typically bring home $100 to $150 worth of groceries. Every time I shop, my goal is to save at least 50% off the retail cost of the groceries. For example, if I go into a store and purchase everything on my grocery list at full price without using a single coupon, I may pay $70. Using the techniques in this book, I am able to bring the total bill for those same groceries down to $35 or less using coupons, sales and other techniques.

**$50 buys my family
$100 to $150 worth of food each week.**

There are even some store promotions, such as coupon doubling or tripling, that allow us to purchase an amazing amount of groceries for very little money. When a grocery store doubles the face value of a coupon it is called "coupon doubling." In coupon doubling, for example, if the face value of a coupon is 50 cents off of a product and the store is doubling coupons, they will increase the value of the coupon to $1 off. When a store triples the amount of the coupon's face value it is known as "coupon tripling." Using the same 50-cent coupon as in the previous example, if the store is tripling coupons, that coupon would then be worth $1.50! You can certainly see how a person can save serious money during these types of promotions.

There are many stores across the United States that double coupons every day. Unfortunately, not all states have stores that offer double coupons, but it is worth your while to find out if you live near any of the stores that do. More information regarding coupon doubling and tripling can be found in the "Coupons" section of this chapter.

During one particular weekend in August 2005, when a national grocery store chain was tripling the face value of coupons (which usually happens every 4-6 months in my area), I purchased $269.78 in groceries and non-food essentials. After coupons were tendered I only owed $4.71. **I paid less than $5 for over $269 worth of groceries!** Needless to say, our pantry was in good shape after that weekend! We also had bags of food, cleaning supplies and health and beauty items to donate to Hurricane Katrina victims the following month because of our August triple coupon bonanza.

Although not everyone has access to stores that double or triple the face value of coupons, you will be happy to know that *this system works no matter where you shop.* Certainly you may save more if coupon doubling and/or tripling are available to you, but I assure you, even without that benefit, your savings can still be substantial with the Smart Spending Grocery System.

Where to Buy Food and Non-Food Essentials

Let's start by exploring the different locations where you can purchase food and non-food staples. Although specific store chains vary from state to state, the concept of store types remains the same. Understanding the types of stores that are available will help you increase your buying power.

Locations for purchasing food and non-food staples fall into seven basic categories:
1. Grocery Stores
2. Drug Stores
3. Warehouse Clubs
4. Mass Merchandisers
5. Dollar-Type Stores
6. Convenience Stores
7. Farmer's Markets/Roadside Stands

Those of you who shop at more than one store each week to target the sales and loss leaders are absolutely getting better deals than the people who only shop one store for all their groceries. You may be thinking that with the price of gas these days, it isn't cost effective to drive farther to shop at another store. Although this may be true if you are picking up only one or two items, it is not the case if a store is offering great sale prices on many items or if a store is doubling or tripling coupons. Keep in mind that you may be able to save $30 or more during a good sale, which is certainly worth the $2 you may spend in gas to get there and back. Bring a friend and share the fuel expense as you take advantage of the excellent buys and loss leaders.

Loss leaders are the items that stores mark down considerably to entice you into their store. They may actually lose money on these items, but they expect you to buy enough additional items to make up for the loss leaders. An example of a loss leader is when a grocery store sells 13 ounce cans of name brand veggies for 25 cents or a dozen eggs for 39 cents. Often, the stores limit the number of loss leaders you can buy in one purchase. You may have to make more than one trip to a store during the sale period if you want to purchase more of the deeply discounted items. Now it's time for further discussion of the 7 places to shop for those loss leaders and all your other grocery and non-food essentials.

Grocery Stores
In the case of food shopping, the obvious holds true; the best place to make the majority of your food purchases is at the grocery store. Most grocery stores offer a decent variety of grocery items and brands, including store brands. Many offer a customer rewards program of some kind (discussed in further detail later in this chapter), which can save you a lot of money when used wisely.

Depending on where you live, you may have many grocery stores to choose from or you may have just one. If you are in an area with at least two grocery stores, you will be able to compare prices and get better deals than if you have only one grocery store available. Even if you have just one option, you can still use sales and coupons effectively to cut your grocery bills.

If you really want to make a dent in your grocery bill, your only loyalty should be to the stores that give you the best deals, and there are some fabulous deals out there at grocery stores! If you have access to a grocery store that doubles or even triples the face value of a coupon, your opportunities for saving increase greatly.

Another issue to consider is the price of gas, which has soared in recent months to new and frustrating highs. When making trips to more than one store, remember to combine those trips with other errands to conserve gas and keep costs down. For example, stop by the grocery store offering great loss leaders on your way home from work or school instead of making a special trip during the weekend.

It is important to remember that you will usually pay more money and have a smaller selection at specialty food stores, such as health food stores. They offer many prepared and hard to find items, which are significantly more expensive than traditional grocery store prices. Specialty food stores often do not carry brands that issue coupons for their products and the savings opportunities are limited when buying at these stores. A box of brand name whole-wheat crackers purchased on sale using a coupon at a grocery store is almost always going to be less expensive than a similar item at the specialty store.

When it comes to grocery store savings, STAY AWAY FROM THE PREPARED DELI AND BAKERY DEPARTMENTS! You can make the delicious pasta salad and baked chicken you see in the deli for a fraction of the cost using your own ingredients. Read more about frugal meals in Chapter 3.

Wondering how to get good deals on fruit and vegetables? Many grocery and warehouse stores have sections for bruised, very ripe or damaged produce that they sell at a reduced price. These "culls", as they are called, are often perfect for a meal that night or the next or can be frozen immediately for use at a later date. If ripe bananas are in the culled section, use them for banana bread or take them out of the peel, freeze them and use them for smoothies.

Drug Stores

Drug stores have carved out a nice little niche for themselves targeting the health, beauty and paper goods market. Recently, they have made an effort to branch out into more food and novelty-related items. Have you noticed the great prices on a gallon of milk at some drug stores? Often, you can find a better price on milk at a drug store than at the grocery store! Take a look at the food section in your local drug store the next time you get a prescription filled. You may be surprised at some of the competitive prices.

Many drug store chains also offer great monthly rebates on all sorts of items, including toothpaste, shampoo, lotion, makeup, bug spray and so much more. Often the rebates are for the full price you paid for a product, making it FREE! All you end up paying is the tax (where applicable) and the cost of the stamp to mail off the rebate. There is much more information about rebates later in this chapter and using them is an excellent way to develop an overstock of free or almost free quality health and beauty essentials.

When you consider the surprising food deals you can find, the ability to use both manufacturer's and store coupons, and the rebates they offer, you can see that drug stores are not just for medicine and mascara anymore!

Warehouse Clubs

Can warehouse clubs save you money? Maybe, if you pay close attention to what you are buying and exercise extreme willpower and diligence when you are shopping.

The number one rule to remember when shopping at a warehouse club is: Be an informed consumer. Take your price book so you can compare the cost per unit of items at the warehouse club to those listed in your price book. A price book is a list of the best deals you have found on the items you regularly buy and it is discussed in the next section of this chapter. Without a calculator and a price book to compare prices, you will never know if that case of 10 cans of tomato sauce really is a better deal per ounce than the cans you can buy individually on sale at your grocery store.

If you are shopping the sales at grocery stores and using coupons, you will probably pay much less per unit (ounce, pound, piece) for food items at grocery stores than at a warehouse club, even if the warehouse club accepts coupons. Some of the best deals at warehouse clubs can be found in the non-food items, including books, clothes and televisions. There are even some good deals on calling cards and cruises at warehouse clubs! Milk is often a good buy at these types of stores as well.

When shopping at a warehouse club, keep in mind that it is very tempting to buy all the convenient, frozen prepared items and giant sized boxes of everything. These purchases do not save you money if you can make the dishes yourself for less or if you can use coupons combined with sales for better-priced packages at the grocery store. Also, keep in mind that the stock varies from week to week at warehouse stores. You can't count on them to always have the same items or the same prices each time you shop.

Visit your local warehouse clubs. Take your price book and calculator and go with a friend who has a membership or ask the person at the door for a guest pass. Compare shelf prices to those in your price book for the types of items you buy. Figure any potential savings. Then, based on your figures, you can decide whether or not to buy a membership. If you find that a warehouse club membership will save you money on the items you buy, consider splitting the membership cost with a friend or family member. Some stores will allow two people to share a membership, cutting your annual cost in half—another smart spending move!

Mass Merchandisers
Mass merchandisers, such the big mart chain stores, offer some good deals on food and non-food items. They have very competitive buys on store brand items, such as garbage bags, paper products and grocery items. Once again, the key is to compare prices per unit. Remember, just because something is in a bigger package does not mean it is a better deal. The large super stores have some good deals on food and if you live in an area where the grocery stores do not double the value of your coupons, these super marts (which also don't double coupons) have some very good buys. Use your price book to compare prices per unit and you won't ever miss a deal!

Many mass merchandisers price-match. If another store in the area offers a lower price on a product identical to one sold by the super mart store, they will sell you the product at the lower price. Make sure you bring in a copy of the ad for the other store that clearly shows the lower price. Call your local store to see if they price-match; it may save you many trips to other stores.

Dollar-Type Stores

Great deals can be found at dollar-type stores when you use manufacturer's coupons. If your local dollar-type store accepts coupons, you will be able to get a number of cleaning, oral care, snack food and paper products inexpensively. Not every chain takes coupons, so call ahead to verify that the dollar-type store in your area does indeed accept manufacturer's coupons. Many of these stores do not accept credit cards.

Convenience Stores

You may be wondering why I have included convenience stores as a place to buy food, but there are many people who use convenience stores as grocers. They run in to grab this or that and, in the end, pay significantly more than they should for basic staples such as milk, cereal and bread. If you are a convenience store shopper, try your best to break this bad habit. Plan your grocery list to include those items you now buy at convenience stores. By planning ahead, you won't be caught without an item and forced to pay inflated convenience store prices.

Farmers Markets and Roadside Stands

During the growing season for your area, if you do not grow your own vegetables and fruits, consider purchasing from your local farmer's market and area roadside stands. You can find wonderfully fresh produce at a wonderfully low price at these locations. For example, the local roadside stand near my home sells locally grown tomatoes for 99 cents per pound during the summer months when they are in season. In contrast, the grocery store down the street sells tomatoes for $2.99 per pound and they do not taste nearly as good. Plus, you will be supporting the local farmers in your area. Many farmers also offer great deals on culls, the damaged, bruised or very ripe items. Ask the seller if there are any available and you may get a bargain.

Developing a Price Book

A price book is simply a list of the items you use regularly and the best prices they sell for in the stores where you are willing to shop. A price book is an excellent tool for tracking prices, sales and buying opportunities. Prices in a price book should be listed by cost per unit so you can easily compare different size packages from different stores. When you see a deal in the weekly flyer or in the store, you will know instantly if it is really a good deal and worth your time to go out and purchase. Just because an item is on sale doesn't automatically make it a good buy. The regular price at some stores may be less than the sale price at others. Your price book is an invaluable tool to help you determine if a sale is really a deal.

 You don't have to create the whole book at once, just carry it with you when you go to the store and write down the best prices when you see them. You can also use the weekly sales flyers and your store receipts to find the best prices. If you make an entry in your price book and then find a better price at another store, change the information to reflect the better deal. After a while you'll have an excellent price record of the things you like to buy. If you add dates to the entries you will begin to see the sale pattern for that item. You don't need to include everything you ever use in the course of a year, just those items you buy regularly. You can price items for as many stores as you want or just the main store at which you shop.

Is it a better deal to buy the largest size of an item or the smallest size? You will be surprised to know that biggest isn't always best! Larger sizes can be more economical than smaller sizes, but that is not usually the case with this system. A smaller size item that is on sale can often be less per unit than the larger size of that same item. When you use a coupon on top of the sale, you can really cut the cost per unit.

Calculating Cost Per Unit: Some stores make it especially hard to figure out cost per unit (ounce, pound, etc.) because they list the prices on the tags as 3/$5.00 or 2/$4.98. First you have to figure out the cost of one of the items and then you have to figure out the cost per unit. You may think this is difficult, but just take a small calculator with you when you shop so you will not have to figure the cost in your head. When stores offer shelf tags with cost per unit clearly indicated, you won't need that calculator.

Sample unit shelf tag:

Your Price $1.99	Unit Price $1.77 Per Pound
18 Ounce Box Of X Brand Cereal Order Number Number of packages per case UPC Number	Barcode

To figure out the cost per unit of an item, follow this simple equation:

Cost of item divided by the **# of units** = **cost per unit**.

Using the shelf tag example above, the equation would look like this: **$1.99** divided by **18 ounces** = **.11 (11 cents)**

In this case, the cost per unit is 11 cents per ounce. When you see this same cereal on sale elsewhere in a different size package, you can easily calculate which package is the better deal. For instance, if a smaller size package of the same product is on sale for $1.15 for a 12-ounce package, you will have enough information to be able to compare the two packages. The 18-ounce package is 11 cents per ounce ($1.99 divided by 18 oz. = 11 cents per ounce). The 12-ounce package is 9.5 cents per ounce ($1.15 divided by 12 oz. = 9.5 cents per ounce). As you can see, the smaller package on sale is a better deal than the larger package at regular price because the cost per ounce of the smaller package is lowest. Often the difference is much more than just a penny per ounce and the savings can add up very quickly.

Some people use a small spiral notebook and write in the prices of the items they use. Others use spreadsheets or word processing software to enter their price book prices. There are even some high tech options such as downloading a price book program into a handheld computer. Your price book can be as short or as long as you wish. You may decide to list the top 20 items you buy regularly or you may decide to create a 10- page list of all the items you buy. How in-depth you make your list is up to you. The key is that it is accurate and that you can reference it easily when you are shopping.

The following price book sample contains details on sale dates, stores and brands, as well as unit price. Some price books only include the item, size and brand and do not get as detailed as this example. Use the blank price book sheet in the appendix to begin creating your price book.

Price Book Sample:

Department: Dairy

Date	Store	Item	Brand	Size	$	Unit Price
4-24	ABC Grocery	Yogurt	Store Brand	8 oz	.50	6 cents per oz
8-23	DEF Grocery	Sour Cream	XYZ Name Brand	16 oz	.99	6 cents per oz
4-14	GHI Grocery	Shred. Cheese	Store Brand	8 oz	.99	12 c./oz

Now, let's take a look at one of the biggest money savers available to grocery shoppers—coupons.

Coupons—The Other Currency

Who really uses all those coupons from the Sunday paper and other sources? According to the Promotion Marketing Association (PMA) Coupon Council, consumers of all age groups, educational backgrounds and income levels redeem coupons. That means shoppers from all walks of life see the benefits of coupon use.

The PMA (http://www.pmalink.org) also reports that at least 74% of Americans use coupons and those consumers save $3 billion per year. Combine that information with the fact that manufacturers offered over $250 billion worth of coupons in 2003 and you can see that only a fraction of the coupons offered were actually redeemed. Manufacturers rely on coupons to bring attention to their products, but they expect that many shoppers will forget to use their coupons, purchasing items at full price.

Coupons are the tools of choice for anyone wanting to stretch their grocery dollars as far as they will go. For those of us who know how to use them effectively, coupons have become like another form of currency. Some of our groceries are paid for with cash, but many of them are purchased with coupons!

You should not be embarrassed about presenting a cashier with a handful of coupons that will save your family 50% or more off of your grocery bill. On the contrary, using coupons effectively is something to be proud of and a skill worth mastering. Once you have begun using this system, you will be amazed at how many people (especially those who are in line behind you at the grocery store) will want to know how you are saving so much! These little pieces of "paper gold" will allow you to stock your pantry and feed your family for a fraction of the full retail price. After a few months, you will find that you have developed an impressive overstock for very little money.

There are 3 types of coupons:

Manufacturer's coupons
Store coupons
Register coupons

A **manufacturer's coupon** is a coupon issued by the maker of the product. They can generally be redeemed at any store that accepts coupons. The most well known place to find these coupons are in FSI's (free standing inserts), which are usually referred to as Sunday supplement coupons, found in your Sunday newspaper. Manufacturer's coupons can also be found at manufacturer Web sites, magazines, direct mailings, coupon displays in your grocery store (you have probably seen the red blinking coupons on the shelves), and many other places. Finding these coupons is discussed in detail later in this chapter.

A **store coupon** has a specific store's name printed on the coupon and can only be redeemed at that store or chain of stores. Store coupons can be found in weekly ads, on displays in the store, through direct mailings and on receipts from purchases made at the store. Manufacturer's and store coupons may be combined at many locations to increase your savings significantly.

In many grocery and drug stores, you can use a store coupon at the same time you use a manufacturer's coupon for the same item.

Yes, many grocery and drug stores will let you use two coupons on the same item, as long as one is a store specific coupon (that does not have "Manufacturer's Coupon" written on it) and the other is a manufacturer's coupon. To find out if your stores will accept both coupons on the same item, all you need to do is ask.

A **register coupon** is a coupon that is printed at the register after you have paid for your purchase. These register coupons are usually white with a red or blue border. You can find them at many grocery stores. Often you will find that the coupon you receive is for a competing brand of a product you just purchased. Sometimes you will even receive coupons for FREE items. Don't throw register coupons away before reading them carefully! These coupons are unusual in that they list a store name and can only be redeemed at that store, but are actually manufacturer's coupons and can't be used in conjunction with other manufacturer's coupons. Most register coupons also state "Not To Be Doubled" which means the value will not be doubled even if the store doubles manufacturer's coupons.

Couponing Tip: When using coupons, make sure that you do not buy products you could purchase less expensively in another brand or make yourself for less. One of the keys to using coupons is to use them wisely, which means not spending extra money on a product you don't use just because you have a coupon. Only use them on products you normally buy or on products that are a great deal that you know you will use or can donate.

Also remember that you do not get to spend more money as a reward for using coupons! The goal here is to save money, not to spend extra on "rewards" for good coupon use.

Doubling and Tripling Coupons
Many stores will redeem your manufacturer's coupons at face value. Fortunately for consumers, there are many stores in the United States that will actually double or even triple the face value of some coupons, increasing savings dramatically. As consumers, we benefit significantly from the competition that prompts stores to offer coupon bonuses such a doubling or tripling!

One of the best ways to increase your savings is to shop at stores that double or even triple the value of your manufacturer's coupons. When a store doubles coupons, a coupon worth 40 cents is actually redeemed for 80 cents at the register. Stores which double and triple coupons have different rules for use depending on the store and the particular sale. Those rules may include only allowing a certain number of different coupons to be doubled or tripled, allowing a maximum number of multiple identical coupons to be doubled or tripled, or requiring a minimum purchase before they will double or triple. You can find out all the details for your stores just by asking at customer service.

> Many stores double coupons every day of the year, which means you can save a bundle every time you go to the store!

Many stores that triple coupons do not offer tripling every day of the year. Some stores only do so a few times a year and that is the time to get stocked up on non-perishables. Check your Sunday and Wednesday sales flyers to see if your stores offer doubling or tripling. If you do not get the ads at your home, go online to the store's Web site (most chains have a national Web site) and look at the sales flyers for your area. If you call customer service at your local stores, they can also explain their coupon policies.

When stores double and triple coupons, you can often purchase items for very little money and sometimes those products are actually free! For example, if your favorite peanut butter is on sale for $1.29 and you have a 60-cent coupon, you will only pay 69 cents for the jar. If the same store doubles coupons with a face value of up to 60 cents, your coupons would then be worth $1.20 and the jar of peanut butter would only cost 9 cents ($1.29 sale price - $1.20 doubled coupon)! Most stores will not give you the difference in cash if your coupons are worth more than the item, but you will get the item at no cost. For example, if your store triples your 60-cent peanut butter coupon, the store will not pay you the difference between the $1.29 sale price and the $1.80 tripled coupon value. But, you will get the item for free! Remember, free is good! If you don't need the free item, consider donating it to a local charity or giving it to a neighbor or friend. Note: in most states, you will pay tax on an item's price before the coupon, even if the item is free with the coupon.

Printed on some coupons are the words *Do Not Double, Do Not Triple, DND or DND-9.* *Do Not Double* means that the coupon should not be doubled, even if the store offers double coupons. *Do Not Triple* indicates that the coupon should not be tripled even if the store triples coupons. *DND* is an abbreviation for *Do Not Double.* *DND-9* is an abbreviation for *Do Not Double* or multiply at all up to nine times. You will find that some stores double coupons even when the coupons indicate *Do Not Double.* It all depends on how your particular store handles coupons and you will have to check with your retailer to confirm their specific policy. Often you will find that coupons whose UPC code starts with the number 5 will double at the register (even if the coupon has *Do Not Double* written on it). Coupons that have a UPC code starting with the number 9 will typically not double.

BOGO
When stores offer Buy One Get One Free (BOGO) deals, there are fantastic opportunities for savings. Some stores ring up a BOGO deal as one full-priced item and one free item. When this happens, most stores will let you use a coupon for the full-priced item but not for the FREE item. When a store allows you use a coupon for the item you are paying for AND one for the free item, the deal is that much better.

During a BOGO sale, some stores will ring up each item at half price and accept a coupon for each of the items. When you are able to use a coupon for each half-priced item the cost per unit goes down drastically! When taking advantage of BOGO deals, try to use coupons whenever you can to get the lowest prices possible.

Free Item With Purchase Offers
There are many techniques that manufacturers use to convince you to buy their products. One of those techniques involves offering a free product if you buy one or more items. For instance, a manufacturer recently offered a coupon for one free national brand bleach product if you buy three other products (at the same time) made by that same manufacturer. Coupons like this can be a good deal if you also use coupons to purchase each of the other products required to get the free item. Because the coupon is for the free item, and not for the required purchases, many stores will let you use cents-off coupons on the required items at the same time as the free product coupon. You would be able to use a coupon for each of the items as well as the coupon to get the fourth item free.

Coupon Organizers

How many times have you seen a good buy but could not find the coupon that you knew was somewhere in your purse or stacked on your kitchen table? You are not alone! The good news is that there are some very effective and manageable ways to organize your coupons that will increase your grocery savings tremendously.

An essential component of the Smart Spending Grocery System is the ability to find your coupons when you need them. There are many ways to organize coupons and there is no one method that is perfect for all couponers. There are some methods that work much better than others, though.

Common coupon organization methods include:

- Accordion-style file
- Envelope in the purse
- A lunchbox or shoebox with dividers
- A small zippered pouch with dividers
- A plastic box made for index or recipe cards
- The binder method

Accordion Style Organizers, Envelopes and Boxes

The organization methods that involve filing coupons one in front of the other make it very difficult to see what you have available. When you are in the store searching for a coupon, you will spend a lot of time flipping through each envelope or section and looking through each stack. It is very easy to let coupons expire with these types of methods because you can't see the coupons easily. The benefits of these types of methods are that the carriers are often small enough to put into your purse and they are usually lightweight.

The Binder Method – The Preferred Organizer

The binder method is the preferred organization method for couponers who want to save the most when using their coupons.

The binder method involves filing coupons in baseball card holders, dividing them by product type and storing them in a three-ring binder. This method takes couponing to a new level of organization and allows the user to take full advantage of available buying opportunities.

Benefits of using the binder method:

• A three-ring binder organizer can hold far more coupons than an accordion file or recipe box organizer.

• Each coupon and its value are visible, cutting down on the time it takes to find a coupon when you are looking over the sales flyers and when you are shopping.

• There is greater potential savings because expiration dates are easier to see and you are less likely to let a valuable coupon expire.

• You can quickly flip to the pages for the section of the store you are in and see all the coupons you have available. This is especially important if you run into an unexpected or unadvertised deal.

• The binders fit easily on the front part of the cart so flipping through the pages as you walk through the aisles is simple.

• These organizers are easily expandable. As your coupon inventory increases, add more coupon pages to your binder.

• Many binders have pockets with room for your sales flyers, calculator, pens and store reward cards.

• The cost of putting together an organizer or buying a Smart Spending Coupon Organizer is easily recovered when you use the Smart Spending techniques, usually after just 1-2 trips to the grocery store.

Create Your Own Binder Coupon Organizer

Supplies needed

- High-quality three-ring zipper binder
- 24 tabbed dividers with clear or colored tabs
- 24 nine-pocket per page baseball card holders, top loading (the opening is at the top of each pocket)
- Calculator
- Pen or pencil
- Small pad of paper

Directions

1. Start with a high-quality three-ring zipper binder. There are many styles and colors available at office supply stores, drug stores and mass merchandisers. Choose an organizer with 1&1/2-inch rings or 2-inch rings, so it is big enough to hold all your coupon pages.

2. Gather 24 tabbed dividers. These can be purchased at the same places you find zipper binders.

3. Gather 24 nine-pocket per page baseball card holders, top loading. These can be found at sports stores and mass merchandisers.

4. Label the tabbed dividers alphabetically by product group. Following are some suggested product groups. You can customize your organizer by changing the product groups to fit your own needs. For instance, if you do not have pets, do not make a label for pet care.

Baby Items	Deodorants	Pasta and Rice
Baking	Feminine Hygiene	Pet Care
Beverages	Frozen Foods	Photos
Breads	Hair care	Produce
Canned Goods	Laundry	Restaurants
Cereals	Meat	Salad Dressing
Cleaning	Oral Care	Snacks
Condiments	Over the Counter	Soap & Body Wash
Dairy	Paper and Plastic	

5. Take your first labeled divider and place it in your binder so it is face down on the left side of the binder. Place one nine-pocket page after the first divider. Continue alternating dividers and nine-pocket pages until you have used them all. As you begin to coupon more, you will want to add 2-4 pocket pages for each product group to accommodate your growing coupon inventory. Your organizer is now ready to fill with all your valuable coupons.

The Smart Spending Coupon Organizer

If you are thinking that creating your own organizer sounds like too much work, consider purchasing a Smart Spending Coupon Organizer. These high quality organizers arrive with the dividers already labeled and all the coupon pages inserted. All you have to do is file your coupons and head to the store to save! There are many colors and styles available and you won't have to go to the trouble of putting one together yourself. Most people find that they easily save the cost of the organizer after just one trip to the grocery store. For more pictures and information, visit http://www.smartspendingandcouponing.com.

The cost of putting together your own organizer will depend on the type of binder you purchase. Binder prices usually range anywhere from $5 to $20 for nylon and cloth binders. For leather binders you will pay much more, which is not a very frugal choice. The tabbed dividers and nine-pocket pages will run approximately $10 to $15 for 24 dividers and 24 pocket pages, depending on the brands you purchase. You will probably spend approximately 2-3 hours purchasing binder supplies, writing or typing binder tabs, and piecing the parts together.

A Smart Spending Coupon Organizer costs $17.99 plus shipping. If you order more than one organizer, they are $16.99 each. The tabs are already labeled, the coupon pages and tabs are inserted, and the organizer arrives assembled and ready to use.

Filling Your Organizer with Coupons

Now that your organizer is assembled, it is time to sort and file your coupons by product type in the easy-to-see clear pocket pages. Each coupon will go into its own pocket, allowing you to see the details of the coupon, including the expiration date.

* Set your organizer aside and get your coupons. Before you place your coupons in the organizer, it is most efficient to sort them by product section. For instance, start a stack of coupons for Baking, one for Beverages, one for Bread, one for Canned Goods, and one for each of the other sections (if you have coupons for those sections). You can sort at the kitchen table or at the coffee table while watching your favorite television show, or anywhere else you find comfortable.

* Once your coupons are sorted by product type, you are ready to file them in the appropriate sections in your organizer. After sorting this way a few times, it takes less and less time and you will see how much easier it makes filing when you can move alphabetically from one product group to the next without having to backtrack.

* Begin filing the coupons starting with those for Baking (if you have any coupons for that section) and going one section at a time until all your coupons are filed. You can choose to file one specific coupon (and any multiples you have of that same coupon) per pocket or use both sides of the clear nine-pocket page and file two different coupons per pocket, allowing for 18 different coupons per page. If you file one coupon per pocket, your pockets will be less full and it will be easier to pull out each coupon. If you file two different coupons (and any multiples of those coupons) per pocket, you will need fewer nine-pocket pages and your binder will be lighter. Either way is fine and it is simply a matter of personal preference. I prefer one coupon (and the multiples) per pocket because it is easier for me to file and remove coupons. When you file the coupons, you will find that some need to be folded in half to fit. It is amazing that manufacturers make some of these coupons so large! Try folding them so that the expiration date and the

coupon value show on the front so you can see all the important information easily.

- You can choose to further organize your coupons within each product group as well. For instance, within the Dairy product group, you can put all the cheese coupons next to each other and all the yogurt coupons next to each other.

- At least once per month, as you file your coupons, remove those coupons that have expired.

Each time you go through the cycle of filing coupons and shopping with your organizer, you will become more efficient and save more and more money. Don't be surprised if other shoppers stop you in the store to marvel at your organization and fantastic savings!

Coupon Sources

In order to cost-effectively purchase large quantities of the products that you use, you will need multiple copies of coupons for those products. Cutting the coupons from one

Sunday paper insert does not give you enough coupons to make a significant dent in your grocery bill. A little extra effort in finding the coupons for those items you use will result in much greater savings at the register.

An important tip to remember is to shop to your market. This means that if you live in an area that never offers double coupons, you want to find coupons with the highest face value, usually 75 cents and up. If you are able to double coupons regularly, look for coupons that are worth close to the highest amount a store will double. For instance, if a store doubles coupons up to 50 cents, look for 50-cent coupons for the items you buy. When doubled, that 50-cent coupon will be worth $1, whereas a 60-cent coupon at that particular store will not be doubled and will only be worth 60 cents.

Let's take a look at the many places that you can find coupons.

Sunday Newspaper Supplement
If you are interested in having a large variety of coupons from different brands and products, the coupons from the Sunday paper are an excellent source. Each week, with the exception of most holidays, there are anywhere from 1-4 sections of coupons in the paper. Remember to ask your friends, family, neighbors and co-workers for their coupons when they are done with them. You will be amazed at how many people do not clip even ONE coupon each week! Don't stop coupon hunting once you get your Sunday coupons, though. There are so many other places to get wonderful coupons for many of the same products that are in your pantry right now.

Coupon Clipping Web Sites
A great way to find multiples of the coupons you use is to order them through a coupon clipping website. These businesses sell the service of finding, clipping and sending

 the coupons to consumers. Clipping services usually charge a 5 to 10 cent clipping fee per coupon plus shipping and handling. Coupons with a higher face value (such as coupons for $1 off or free items) will have a higher clipping fee. Many sites have a minimum order amount (such as $3) and a minimum of each coupon that you must order (such as 5 of the same coupon). Some do not have any minimums at all. The minimum requirements should not be a problem for most since, with the Smart Spending Grocery System, it is not that difficult to use five copies of a coupon before it expires. Even if you just use one of the five coupons and it is doubled, you have saved far more than the 25-50 cents you spent to get all five of the coupons sent to you.

Many coupon clipping services are small businesses with no employees other than the owner. Often, they only get 100-200 multiples of the weekly coupons from the paper and they sell out quickly. There are a few larger clipping services that consistently have the best selection of coupons available. One such service is The Coupon Clippers (TCC) at http://www.thecouponclippers.com. TCC is reliable, easy to use, well run and well organized. They do an excellent job of maintaining the website with the most current coupons available. A stay-at-home mom and her small coupon clipping staff run the service, based in Florida. According to their Web site, TCC is a "full-service coupon clipping service, providing manufacturer's coupons and rebate forms as well as notices of the items that are on sale at the stores for a small handling fee." For a $4 coupon clipping order, you can achieve approximately $30 or more in savings at the grocery stores. If those coupons are doubled or tripled, your grocery savings will be much higher!

Be aware that some coupon clipping sites charge you just to look at what coupons and rebates are available. These companies typically impose an annual fee to use their service, whether or not you even order from them. Paying a company just to have the option to look at what coupons are available is not a good use of your money.

Friends, Neighbors, Co-workers, Family
Once again, ask all your friends, family, neighbors and co-workers to share their coupons when they are done with them. You will be pleasantly surprised at the number of people who give you full coupon sections from their Sunday paper. You will often receive entire Sunday supplements just by asking!

Coupon Swap
Once you are finished cutting the coupons from your paper each week, you can give the unused coupons to one of your neighbors or friends. You could also ask everyone to bring their coupon inserts to work each week and leave them in a basket for others to go through.

Manufacturer Toll-Free Phone Numbers
By simply calling the toll-free numbers on the packages of the products you eat, you can receive lots of manufacturer's coupons for products you use all the time. When you call manufacturers, let them know that you love their products and would like to purchase them more often, but that you need to use coupons in your shopping. Politely ask if they are able to send out any coupons for the products that you use. You will be surprised at how often companies will send cents-off coupons. Sometimes they will even send a coupon for a free product! These coupons are certainly worth the 5 minutes you will spend on the phone.

Manufacturer Web Sites
Another way to find manufacturer's coupons is on manufacturer's Web sites. Most have a "Promotions" or

"Offers" link. Click on the link and check to see if any printable coupons are offered. You can also click on the "Contact Us" link to let the company know how much you love its product and request any coupons they would be willing to send. If you prefer to speak with someone, you can find the company's phone number, which is usually toll-free, on its Web site, and call to request a coupon. To view a large list of product manufacturers and their websites, see the list at http://www.recipelink.com/companies.html. If you call 2 to 3 companies a week, your mailbox will be full of useful coupons at no cost to you, other than the time it takes to make a toll-free phone call.

Grocery Store Web Sites
Many grocery stores have coupons that they offer to customers who have signed up for their rewards cards. Go to the Web sites for the grocery stores in your area and look to see if they have coupons you can print right from the site. Some grocery stores also send coupons through the mail when you are signed up with their rewards program.

Coupon Web Sites
There are many places online to find printable coupons. Valuable coupons can be found every month at http://www.smartsource.com and http://www.coupons.com. In order to print these coupons, you must first register at the site and sometimes you will be instructed to download a coupon printing software program. Be aware that some stores no longer accept coupons that have been printed on home computers due to the rise in coupon fraud. Before you start searching the Internet for coupons, ask your local stores if they accept coupons printed from the Internet so you will know if it is worth your time to find and print them.

Snail Mail Manufacturer Request
There are times when you are not able to find a manufacturer's phone number or e-mail address, or you

would prefer to send a mailed request. Manufacturers love to receive positive letters about their products and you will find that often they reward the writers of such letters by mailing them wonderful coupons. Remember that you are paying the cost of a stamp to send the letter and that you may not always receive coupons in return. Following is a sample letter to use when you write a manufacturer to request coupons:

(Company Name and Company Address)

Hello,

I am writing to let you know that we really enjoy using (name of product). (Write a few things you like about the product or how it helped in a specific situation, such as an illness.)

If possible, I would very much like to receive coupons and/or samples of your products if they are available. I would also like to be added to your mailing list for future newsletters, coupons and samples. Thank you for your high quality product!

Sincerely,

(your name, address and e-mail)

In-Store Coupon Containers
Have you ever seen those in-store coupon holders that stick out from the shelves? You might be surprised to know that many of these coupons will get you a good deal if you hold on to the coupon and wait for the item to go on sale (especially a buy-one-get-one-free sale). Don't just look for the red coupon holders on the shelves. Look for coupons on the larger floor displays, as well. Another great in-store location to find coupons are the end-cap and shoulder-cap displays. End-caps are the displays at the very end of the

aisle. Often, there are displays hanging from the shelves of end-caps with coupon tear pads. When you come around the corner of an end-cap, you have reached the shoulder-cap. This is the area just behind the end-cap and another place that stores place displays or hanging coupon tear pads.

Online Auction Sites

Another good place to find coupons is at an online auction site, such as E-bay (http://www.ebay.com). When you go to an online auction site, simply type in the specific brand of coupon you want in order to see current auctions for that coupon. For instance, if you are looking for juice coupons, type "juice coupon" into the search box on the auction website. You will often have many choices to consider. If you want to see what different types of coupons are available for a wide variety of products, type "food coupons" into the search box and see what comes up.

Remember to check the shipping and handling costs for these auctions. Some sellers choose to make their profit in shipping and handling costs and start the auction bids very low. You may think you are getting a great deal, but if the shipping and handling fee is high, the cost to have the coupons sent to you may not be such a good use of your money after all.

Local Coupons

Many cities and towns have local coupon mailers that are sent to your home every few months. If your first inclination is to throw them out unopened, think again. There are often very good coupons for restaurants, dry cleaning, oil changes and other local services.

Rain Checks and Substitutes

If you find that a store is sold out of a sale item, ask for a "rain check." A rain check entitles you to get the item at the sale price at a later date, when it is in stock again.

Usually, rain checks are valid for at least 30 days after they are issued and some rain checks have no expiration date at all. You can wait until you have a good manufacturer's coupon to use with your rain check and create your own great deal! Ask the store to issue the rain check for multiples of the item (10 boxes at the sale price, for instance). You can then find/order enough coupons to purchase more than one of the item if it is a very good deal. When you go to redeem the rain check, it's okay if you decide not to get all ten items for which the rain check is issued. The store will not require that you buy all ten to get the sale price.

Sometimes, when a store is out of an advertised item, it will offer a substitute item at the same sale. Hopefully you will have a coupon for the item they are substituting so you can still get an excellent buy. Even if they offer a substitute item, request a rain check for the out-of-stock item and use it later with your coupon.

All Around Town
If you find yourself out at breakfast or lunch on a Sunday morning, take a look at the newspapers that previous diners have left behind. You will find many coupon inserts. Your local library may be willing to give you their coupon inserts from the previous Sunday's paper, as well.

Look On Your Receipts
Look on the bottom and back of receipts from drug stores and grocery stores. You may be surprised to find a coupon or two.

Recycling Bins
If you have access to a newspaper recycling container at your apartment building, pull out the coupon inserts from discarded Sunday papers. You will probably find that many have not even been looked at and that the coupon inserts are completely intact. I should probably clarify that

I am not advocating dumpster diving in nasty garbage cans. Rather, I am encouraging checking in clean receptacles that are used strictly for newspapers.

Questionable Coupon Deals and Booklets

Unfortunately, there are coupon "deals" out there that you need to be aware of. One in particular is a program that requires you to buy certificates for coupons that may be ordered at a later date. When you go to redeem your $10 coupon certificate for brand name coupons, you may only be allowed to choose the brands you would like, not the specific coupon amounts or expiration dates. Once your coupons arrive, you may realize that you have received a fraction of the coupons you ordered, which are often at a low face value or close to expiration. Don't be fooled by offers that do not clearly indicate what you are getting for your money.

Now that your coupon organizer is full of valuable coupons for all the products you use, let's move on to combining those coupons with other techniques to get your grocery bill as low as it can go!

Using Weekly Sale Flyers

All of the major grocery stores, drug stores and mass merchandisers issue weekly sale flyers to highlight the items on sale each week. Different stores start sales on different days, so it is important to know when a sale starts and ends for specific stores. Most stores start their new sales on either Sundays or Wednesdays. If you are ordering coupons online, you want to make sure that you order early enough in the sales cycle to receive your coupons before the sale is over. Sale flyers can be found in local newspapers, in your mailbox, online at store Web sites and at the various stores themselves. Some stores will even mail you a copy of their weekly sales flyer if you call their toll-free number and ask them to do so.

When purchasing sale items, be careful to purchase exactly the items that qualify for the sale price. Sometimes a store will only offer a sale price on certain flavors of an item and not on others. An example would be when red grapes are on sale for 99 cents a pound and white grapes are still $2.99 per pound. Sometimes, the full-priced white grapes are on the same display with the sale-priced red grapes. The sign indicating which item is on sale is not always easily seen and you will pay a hefty price if you grab the wrong grapes.

Another sales tactic to be aware of is quantity requirements. Some stores will offer sales such as buy four of an item and get a sale price of $2 (50 cents each). If you only buy two of the product, you may be charged full price, not the sale price. Some stores, though, will honor the sale price even if you do not purchase the quantity quoted in the sales flyers. All you need to do is ask customer service if you have to buy the quantity required by the ad to get the sale price or if you will also get the sale price if you only buy one of the item.

The Weekly Sale Flyer
Once you have your sale flyers together for the weekly sales, look through the flyers for each store at which you are able to shop. Write down the sale items that you are interested in at each store, as well as the sale price. While you are looking at the flyers, take out your price book, if needed, to see if a sale is really as inexpensive, or even less expensive, than the lowest price that you can find somewhere else. Take out your coupon book and pull out the coupons for the products on your list. You won't have coupons for everything, but you should have them for many of the loss leaders and sale items you purchase.

Once you have decided which stores you will shop at for the week, you can add to your list the items you still need that were not in the sale flyer. The goal is to purchase the foods your family eats on sale and with coupons when possible.

> The key is to buy the loss leaders and sale items in conjunction with a coupon.

The exception is buying store brand items that might be less expensive than national brand items (especially if they are not on sale and you do not have a coupon). Plan your menu for the week around that week's sales and what you already have in your stocked pantry. Shopping for fresh foods that are in season is a great way to cut produce expenses. An even better way to cut produce expenses is to grow your own fruits and vegetables. See Chapter 3 for more information on gardening.

Stock up: Even if you don't need an item that you see on sale, if it is an excellent deal, buy as many as you can justify. Purchasing non-perishables at deep discounts is the ideal way to develop an impressive overstock for much less than you would pay at full price. There are many items, such as milk and bread, that freeze very well, so stock up when the buys are amazing! Remember to only buy products you will use (or donate) before they expire.

An orderly list: Another helpful hint is to write the items on your grocery list in the same order that you find them in the store. This saves time and prevents backtracking to find something at the bottom of the list. If you organize your coupons in the same order as your list, they will be easier to find if you need to check something on the coupon. If you are not very familiar with the store layout, make your list in alphabetical order.

Some stores offer a store layout sheet that lists which products are on which aisles. Ask customer service at the stores you shop if they offer this helpful information.

Flexibility equals savings: Another issue to consider is brand loyalty. Most of us have preferences regarding which brands we like for certain items. For instance, you may only like a certain brand of yogurt that you have been eating for years. If you have tried other brands, including the store brand, and none compare to your favorite, then that is fine. With this system, you can still buy your favorite brands. You just won't save as much as you would if you were flexible enough to use other brands as well. Flexibility means that one week you may be eating one brand of yogurt and the next you may be buying the competing brand because it is better priced.

One of the fun things about being flexible is that you will try many new brands and products and will probably find some new favorites. The most important part, though, is that you have saved so much money!

Using Your Coupon Organizer While Shopping

Once you have made your list, head to the grocery store, but DO NOT forget your coupon organizer and price book! Bringing your coupons into the store will save you even more on unadvertised sales and clearance items.

When you get to the store, place your coupon organizer on the front part of the cart so you can easily see your coupons. If you have a child with you who needs to sit in the front part of the cart, move your organizer to the basket and lay it out there. As the basket fills with groceries, put the organizer on top of the boxes and cans in the cart so you can continue to see the coupon pages easily.

When you put an item in your cart, place the coupon for that item in one of the pockets in the inside or outside cover of your organizer. Once the cashier has scanned your items, you can hand him or her your stack of coupons and you will not be flustered trying to find your coupons. As you go through the aisles and shop from your list, look for sale prices on all the items you buy. There are many products that are on sale but not advertised in the flyer. Don't get caught wishing you had your coupons so you could take advantage of a fantastic unadvertised sale.

Frequent-Shopper Programs

Almost every store now has a free rewards program of some kind for their customers. The way each program works varies from store to store, but they all offer better prices when you use their rewards cards. You will need to sign up for a frequent-shopper card for each store at which you shop. You can carry the cards on your key-chain (if they have the key-chain size cards) or in your wallet, purse or coupon organizer. It is important that you remember to give the cashier your rewards card each time you make a purchase. Some stores give you the best sale prices only when you use your rewards card. Many stores offer extra coupons and offers for rewards card members, so keep your eyes open for store coupons in your mailbox and e-mail.

When you are traveling, don't assume you have to pay higher prices just because you don't have a store rewards card for the grocery store you visit while on vacation. If you are able to prepare some of your own meals while traveling, you will probably be stopping at a few grocery stores along the way. Make sure you sign up for the store rewards card while you are there so you can take advantage of the sale prices while you shop. Even if you do not live anywhere near that store, and will probably never shop there again, you can still sign up for the card. It only takes a minute to fill out the form and you may save $5 or more on just one shopping trip by using your rewards card.

You should be aware that grocery stores benefit from the rewards cards as well. When you first sign up for a card, the store collects demographic information about you, such as your address and age. Each time you use that card, they are able to track what you have purchased. Stores and manufacturers use this information to determine which products to carry, what items to put on sale and what demographic groups to cater to. For example, if a large percentage of shoppers at a particular grocery store are over the age of 55, that store may not carry every single child's cereal or brand of baby food available on the market. Not everyone is comfortable giving stores access to his or her shopping habits and personal information. Certainly, you can decide not to sign up for and use a rewards card. If that is your choice, however, you will not be able to take advantage of sales or double coupon offers, in most cases.

Upromise
http://www.upromise.com

Upromise is a free program that allows you to earn college savings when you purchase qualifying products. First, you set up an account at http://www.upromise.com and register as many of your grocery and drug store rewards cards and credit cards as you wish. Once your cards are registered, every time you purchase a qualifying product or service, you earn up to 10% back for college from thousands of participating companies. The list of qualifying products and the companies who support Upromise can be seen on the Web site. They include major name brands that you more than likely purchase many times a month. You can also earn savings for the account through online purchases, travel, dining out and many other ways.

The account can be opened for your own children, grandchildren, relatives, friends or even for yourself! You can see your account balance online at any time. It is an easy way to save a little more for college. Just keep purchasing the items you already buy!

Frequent Shopper Warning

Be aware of deals that offer you a free gift or gift card if you spend a certain amount of money for a certain number of weeks. If you only spend $30/week at a store and the deal requires that you spend $50, you are not saving money if you spend an extra $20 per week for 6 weeks just to get a $10 bonus. If you qualify for one of the promotions because you already shop at the store and spend the amount required to receive the toaster or ham, then, by all means, enjoy your freebie!

There is an exception to this warning, though. Sometimes, when stores offer a freebie with a certain amount of purchases, they allow you to include gas or stamps in the total purchases required to qualify for the freebie. For instance, let's say that your grocery store is offering a $10 store gift card if you spend $50 per week for the next 8 weeks. That same store also has a gas station and will count gas purchases toward the $50 weekly required minimum. If the gas prices at this store are reasonable, you may be able to earn the $10 gift card very easily by filling up on gas and buying the good deals from that store each week for the duration of the promotion. If stamps are counted toward the minimum purchase requirement, the promotion period would be a good time to stock up for your holiday card mailing and also earn a $10 gift card, just for buying stamps you know you will use in December.

Buying Store Brands

Buying store brand products is an excellent way to save money with every shopping trip. Companies have worked hard to improve their private-label brands and often the taste is equal to the national brands. If you are not already a store brand user, be brave and try a few store brand items. They are often around 20% less expensive than the national brands of the same products. All store brands are not created equal, though. The store brand cottage cheese from one grocery store may not taste as good to you as the store brand from another. Test various products from various stores and make up your own mind.

Remember, if a national brand is on sale and you have a coupon, preferably one that is doubled or even tripled, the price may be much less expensive than the store brand. Keep that in mind when deciding between a store brand product and a national brand product.

Using Rebate Offers

Companies use rebates to persuade consumers to purchase items. They have found that many people who buy rebate items do not follow through with sending in the rebate form and required documentation. People often forget about the rebate completely, let the rebate period expire, or decide they do not want to make the effort to fill out the form even after they have purchased the product. For those of us who do take the time to fill out these easy forms, the savings that rebates offer are tremendous!

You can find rebate forms in the Sunday newspaper coupons, store displays, magazines, manufacturer Web sites and product packages. Once you buy an item, you are usually instructed to send in the completed rebate form, the UPC code from the package and the original or copy of the store receipt. Many rebates require that you circle the item and cost on a receipt and send part of the package as proof of purchase. It is your responsibility to follow the rebate instructions exactly as required in order to receive the rebate.

Between store sales and using manufacturer's coupons and rebates, you can often get items for free! The degree to which people use rebates depends on how much time and energy they want to devote to the activity.

Tips to remember when claiming a mail-in rebate:

- While in the store, pick up or ask for two rebate forms, in case you make a mistake while filling one out.

- Before you buy, make sure the rebate has not expired.

- Read the instructions carefully, read them again, and make sure you do exactly what is written. If you miss one detail, the company can reject your request for a rebate.

- Always photocopy everything, including the rebate coupon, the store receipt and the UPC code from the box.

- The typical wait time is 6 to 8 weeks to receive a rebate check. Keep a small rebate file and list when a rebate was sent, where it was sent, company name, how much the rebate is for, and the time period in which you should receive the rebate check. When you receive a check, mark it off the rebate list. Each month, look to see if there are any rebates that are 2-3 weeks late in processing. If you find a late rebate, contact the company to check on the status.

You will find that using rebate and refund forms is a very inexpensive way to try a product you've never used before. You can also use rebates to develop a good-sized overstock on things you use every day like toothpaste, toothbrushes, deodorants, batteries, shampoo and shaving razors. Many drug stores have excellent rebates on these items every month. Call the drug stores in your area to see if they offer a monthly rebate program.

Watching the Scanner

While the cashier is ringing up your items and coupons, watch the prices as they ring. As we all know, items have been known to ring up incorrectly and it is often easier to correct the mistake before you have paid. Also make sure you watch as your coupons are being scanned. Sometimes a cashier may accidentally miss a coupon or it may not scan correctly. If the store doubles coupons, make sure that the coupons are doubling correctly, as well.

Reviewing the Receipt

Some grocery stores have a price-scan guarantee, so make sure you check your receipt before you leave the store. If you catch the store overcharging you on an item compared

 to the shelf or sale price, which does happen, go to the customer service desk **after** the sale has been completed and you have paid for your groceries. If your store has a price-scan guarantee, you will usually be refunded the full price you paid for the item and you will get to keep the item! Do not leave the store until you have looked over every item on the receipt to make sure you were not overcharged. Stores that do not offer a price scan guarantee will reimburse you for the difference between the correct price and the price they charged you. Some stores will even give you a set amount of money back ($3, for example) if you find that they overcharged you on an item.

Speaking Your Mind

When you find that a product does not meet your standards, it is important to let the manufacturer know about your dissatisfaction. Informing a manufacturer about your discontent regarding a product or the packaging is helpful to the company because it lets them know if there is a manufacturing problem. It can also inform them if a product is not being handled appropriately during delivery and storage. Often, the manufacturer will send you a coupon to replace the item that was not satisfactory.

Keep in mind that you don't have to wait until you have a negative experience with a product to contact a manufacturer. If you are pleased with a product, write them a note or give them a call with your positive comments and then politely request any coupons they could possibly send. They will often send you multiple coupons for the products they sell.

Understanding Store Tactics

Every grocery store hopes that you will do most, if not all, of your shopping at their location. Many use tactics that entice the shopper to stay longer and buy more. It is important for you to understand what those tactics are and avoid being taken by them. Remember that these tactics are not evil techniques designed to drain your bank account of every dollar and leave you flailing financially. Marketing to increase sales is their job. Your job is to learn the skills that allow you to make wise choices that are not influenced by clever marketing. Following are some methods stores use to get you to spend your money at their location:

What's That Wonderful Smell?!: Stores bake fresh bread, cookies, chicken, and all sorts of tasty prepared foods right there in the store. The smell of those items is often enough to get you to buy whatever it is they are cooking. Once again, STAY AWAY FROM THE PREPARED DELI FOODS and your grocery bill will not burst your well-prepared budget!

Store Layout: Stores often put the more expensive brand-name products at eye-level, where they will be easily seen. To find the store brand and clearance items, you need to look on the higher and lower shelves.

Is It Really on Sale?: Be aware that stores often place non-sale items on the same fancy display as sale items. Their hope is that you will pick up both items, especially if the non-sale item is usually used with the sale item, such as ketchup with hot dog buns.

Package Size: Bigger is not always better. When a store has a monster size package of an item you want to purchase, remember that just because something is packaged in a larger box or a multi-pack does not mean that you are getting a better deal. Remember to figure out the price per unit to see which size package is the best buy.

Checkout Lines: If you have children, try to stay away from the checkout lines with candy or toys. It will cut down on the whining and begging from your children and the impulse shopping you may do just to appease them. The same thing goes for adults who have a weakness for chocolate!

How Much Time Does This Really Take?

You are probably wondering if I spend 10 hours a day ordering, sorting and filing coupons, going through sale flyers, making a grocery list, and actually going to the stores to shop for my family. The truth is that I DO NOT spend every waking hour couponing and shopping. I do take it seriously, though, because these techniques save our family a substantial amount of money.

With that said, you should be able to clip, sort and file coupons during your favorite evening TV shows and while watching your little one at ballet class. Plan on another 15 minutes for ordering coupons online. Once your coupons are filed, you will probably spend another 30 minutes looking through the sales ads and writing your shopping list. I usually do one larger shop per week and one or two other quick trips to stores with great loss leaders. My larger shop (where I spend $30 or so) takes about 1 hour. The 1-2 quick trips take about 15 minutes each and are made while running other errands.

If you add up the numbers you will get a total of approximately three to four hours per week spent on grocery planning and purchasing. Is it worth it? Let's say you used to spend $140 per week on groceries and non-food essentials before you read this book. Then you started using the Smart Spending Grocery techniques and cut your grocery bill down to $70 per week. That is a savings of $70 per week, which equals $3640 per year. Is three and a half hours of planning and shopping a week worth $3640 over the course of a year? Close your eyes for a moment and imagine what you could do with an extra $3640 each and every year!

What if the Deals Are Amazing?

Staying within your weekly grocery budget is very important to the financial stability of your family. With that said, it is acceptable to spend slightly more then your budget dictates one week if the sales are amazing and you are able to stock up on items at rock bottom prices. During the next 2-3 weeks, though, you will need to adjust your budget to make up for the overage. I look at my grocery budget on both a weekly and a monthly level. My goal is to stay under $50 per week every week. When I find an exceptional sale and decide to add to my overstock or have another valid reason to go over my budget (big family affair, for instance), I am careful not to go over the total food budget of $200 per month.

Key Points To Remember

- Flexibility equals savings. If you are able and willing to shop at more than one store each week, you can take advantage of the sales and loss leaders that the various stores have to offer.

- A Price Book lists the lowest prices for the items you buy regularly. Use this tool to make sure you are paying an acceptable price per unit every time you shop.

- Using coupons in conjunction with sales can increase savings significantly. Use the many resources available to find coupons for the items you use.

- Organize your coupons so you can see them clearly and access them easily, especially while in the grocery store. The preferred method is the three-ring binder system.

- Use the weekly sale flyers when making your grocery list and don't forget your coupons and price book while shopping.

- Rebates, store rewards cards, store brands, price scan guarantees and unadvertised sales can all save you money at the register. Consider these tools each time you shop.

- Stores and manufacturers use very successful marketing to entice shoppers to buy more. Be aware and don't get taken by tactics designed to increase your grocery bill.

- If you follow the techniques in the Smart Spending Grocery System, you will cut your grocery bills significantly and still continue to eat the meals you are accustomed to enjoying.

Key Actions to Take

You have all the pieces to the money-saving and couponing puzzle for grocery shopping. Let's put them together.

1. Start by creating a price book and a coupon organizer.

2. Go to the local grocery and drug store chains or go their Web sites and sign up for the rewards cards.

3. Gather the weekly sale flyers for the stores you will shop at and make a list of the loss leaders and sale items you wish to purchase. Pull out the coupons you will use in combination with the sale items.

4. Buy the loss leaders and sale items with coupons, if applicable, at the stores with the best deals. Also, do not forget your calculator, coupon organizer and price book so you can take advantage of any unadvertised sales.

5. Reserve your larger shop for the store with the best deals on the items you need. Shop from your list, use coupons combined with sales, buy store brands, and use the store rewards card.

6. Pay with a credit card that offers rewards of some kind, such as airline miles or cash back bonuses, as long as you pay your credit card bill in full each month.

7. Look over your receipt for any errors. Approach customer service for the price-scan guarantee if you find an error.

8. Track your expenditures and savings so you can see how much hard earned money you are saving!

Chapter 3

Frugally Fed

Now that you have learned how to cut your grocery expenses, you can focus on being frugal with those groceries you purchased at such great deals!

Meal Planning

Creating frugal meals begins with meal planning. Meal planning simply involves deciding ahead of time what you will be eating for the week or month. In addition to the reduced cost of meals, meal planning offers the benefit of stress reduction. How many times have you come home after a long day and wondered what in the world you were going to cook that night for dinner? How many times have you simply given up and ordered an expensive pizza instead of tackling your oven? Meal planning takes the stress and the guesswork out of the kitchen and allows you to enjoy homemade, healthy options most nights of the week. One of the best ways to plan meals is to develop a Master Meal List and use that list to create a weekly menu based on what is on sale that week and what you already have in your pantry.

The Master Meal List: Meal planning begins with making a thorough list of the meals your family likes to eat. Involve everyone in the house so they will have a chance to give input about their favorite and least favorite meals. Place this master list in a three-ring binder and keep it accessible. You will want to reference it each week and amend it to add new dishes that work for your family. Once the master list is made, it is time to plan your weekly menu.

The Weekly Menu: Each week, determine what meals you will serve using items in your pantry and items that are on sale. Choose five meals from your master list and add them to your calendar, indicating which meal you will eat on which night. Leave two nights open so you can finish off leftovers or have a meal that doesn't involve a lot of cooking, such as sandwiches. Make sure you offer a good variety in the foods you are serving from day to day so your frugal menus will be well received. The meals do not have to be difficult and many can be made ahead of time and pulled from the freezer. Make sure you spend time each night preparing for the next day's meal. Decide whether you need to pull out food from the freezer, cook ingredients in the crockpot, or cut vegetables for the stew that will be cooking in the crockpot the next day.

Sample Frugal Meals

- Crockpot beef and noodles, homemade bread, fresh fruit

- Lasagna, salad, garlic bread

- Chicken or beef quesadillas, rice, canned peaches

- Grilled cheese sandwiches, vegetable soup, fresh fruit

- Tuna noodle casserole with broccoli, biscuits, applesauce

- Egg and cheese rolled-up in a tortilla, fruit

- Yogurt with granola, muffin, banana

Ideas for Every Meal

There are many frugal ways to serve breakfast, lunch, dinner and snacks. With a little preparation and smart shopping, you can serve a healthy, hearty and tasty meal for a fraction of the full retail cost.

Breakfast

- Turn to your freezer for homemade pancakes, muffins or breakfast burritos you have made ahead and frozen. Serve your pancakes with a glass of juice and a serving of fruit and breakfast is taken care of.
- Buy cereal only when it is on sale and you have a coupon. Try not to pay more than $1.50 per box and turn to generic brands when the national brand is not on sale. When you find your favorite cereal for 50 cents or less using coupons and sales, stock up.
- Omelets are an inexpensive way to use leftover meats and vegetables. Serve with a piece of toast and jelly.
- Whip up a fruit smoothie with ice, yogurt, milk and fruit for a filling, tasty and healthy treat.
- Serve oatmeal with fresh fruit.

Lunch

- Eat the leftovers from the previous night's dinner for lunch. Put the leftover meat on salad or a tortilla or pita bread for a delicious sandwich. Add fresh carrot sticks and a piece of fruit and lunch is served.
- Add extra macaroni to your too-cheesy mac and cheese to double your meals.
- Tried and true PB & J always works. Try some variations like peanut butter and banana.
- A bowl of soup and a piece of wheat bread taste great on a cold winter day.
- Tuna salad and egg salad are good frugal options. Stuff the salad into a slightly hollowed out homegrown tomato and you have a delicious and inexpensive lunch.

- Make your own packaged lunch tray including cheese, crackers, grapes, carrots and a few thin slices of turkey.
- Use tortillas to roll up just about any sandwich filling including deli meats (purchased on sale, of course), tuna, egg salad, cream cheese with sliced cucumbers and tomatoes, or hummus.
- Make thin crust personal pizzas using tortillas. Everyone loves them because they get to choose their own toppings. Bake at 450 degrees for 5-7 minutes.
- For school lunches, go to a dollar store and purchase the individual smaller-sized plastic containers. Use them to hold dips like peanut butter and salad dressing. They are also great for pudding, fruit salad or cut vegetables.

Dinner
- Since meats are usually the most expensive part of a meal, stretch your meats by using extra veggies, grains or beans. If you do this slowly, your family will barely notice the difference and you will end up saving significantly on your meat purchases.
- Use the crockpot to soften tougher, less costly meats.
- Enjoy meatless meals. Serve a spinach and mushroom pizza or meatless lasagna.
- When you make a dish that freezes well, triple the batch. Eat one batch that night. Put the extra batches in two separate containers, label them and put them in the freezer. You will develop a nice selection of freezer meals for your weekly meal plan.
- Eat breakfast for dinner, including omelets or a breakfast casserole made with leftover meat and vegetables.
- Offer sandwich night with a varied selection of sandwich fillings, such as tuna salad, egg salad, leftover meat, or an assortment of vegetables and cheese.
- Tuna casserole is always a good frugal favorite.
- Make homemade pizzas using homemade dough and fresh garden vegetables. Delicious and nutritious.
- Have soup and grilled cheese sandwich night.

Frugal Dinner Recipes

Tuna and Noodle Casserole

This is an easy recipe that appeals to the whole family.

3 cups egg noodles
½ medium onion
1 (6 oz.) can tuna fish, drained and flaked
1 can (10 ¾ oz.) condensed cream of mushroom soup
½ cup milk
8 oz. frozen chopped broccoli, thawed in microwave
2 cups shredded cheddar cheese
½ tsp. salt
1 tsp. garlic powder
¼ tsp. black pepper
½ cup flake cereal, crushed

Cook noodles as directed on package, adding onion during the last 1 minute of boiling. Drain noodles and onion. Mix tuna, soup, milk, broccoli, cheese and seasonings in a 2-quart casserole dish. Combine noodles and tuna mixture. Sprinkle top with cereal. Bake uncovered at 375 degrees for 25 minutes or until thoroughly heated. Makes 6 servings. Healthy revisions: Reduce calories and fat by using a reduced fat soup, 1% milk and low fat cheese. Use a can of peas or mixed vegetables instead of broccoli, if desired.

Cost Analysis of Tuna Casserole

Ingredient	Cost
8 oz. wide egg noodles, cooked & drained	50 cents with coupon
½ medium onion	20 cents
1 (6 oz.) can tuna fish, drained	19 cents with coupon
1 can (10 ¾ oz.) condensed cream of mushroom soup	35 cents on sale with coupon
1 cup milk	20 cents
8 oz. frozen chopped broccoli	50 cents on sale
2 cups shredded cheddar cheese	99 cents on sale
½ tsp. salt	2 cents (approx)
1 tsp. garlic powder	2 cents (approx)
¼ tsp. black pepper	3 cents (approx)
½ cup flake cereal, crushed	30 cents on sale
Total Casserole Cost	**$3.30**

Add biscuits made from scratch or Bisquick (free after sale and coupon, of course) and applesauce (purchased on sale) and your meal will cost less than $4 for a family of four!

Crockpot Beef and Noodles

I have made this recipe many times and we all love the tender beef and creamy sauce on noodles. By doubling the recipe, you make this a nice dish for entertaining.

1 pound beef stew meat, trimmed and cubed
4 oz. fresh button mushrooms, quartered
½ onion, chopped
1 clove garlic, minced
2 carrots, sliced
1 tsp. dried oregano
½ tsp. black pepper
1 bay leaf
1 can (14 oz.) beef broth
8 oz. sour cream
½ cup all-purpose flour
¼ cup water
8 oz. wide egg noodles, cooked and drained

Combine beef, mushrooms, onion, garlic, carrots, oregano, pepper and bay leaf in crockpot. Pour in beef broth. Cover and cook on LOW for 8-10 hours or on HIGH for 4-5 hours.

Remove bay leaf and throw away. If cooking on LOW, turn temperature to HIGH. Mix sour cream, flour and water in a bowl. Add 1 cup of liquid from the crockpot into sour cream mixture. Pour sour cream mixture slowly back into crockpot and stir. Cover and cook on HIGH for approximately 30 minutes, until thickened and bubbly. Serve over cooked noodles. Makes 4 servings.

Serve with homemade bread or a crusty wheat bread and fruit for dessert and you have a hearty, healthy meal.

This recipe makes a thick stew sauce. For thinner stew sauce, add 2 cans of beef broth instead of one.

Easy Quesadillas
This is a delicious and easy recipe for making good use of leftover meat.

1 pound cooked boneless chicken or cooked ground beef
¼ packet taco seasoning
8 soft flour tortillas, burrito size
8 oz. package of shredded cheese

Spray a large baking sheet with non-stick spray. Place two tortillas side by side on the baking sheet. Place ¼ of the chicken or beef on each tortilla. Lightly sprinkle the taco seasoning on top of meat. Cover meat with ¼ of the cheese and then place another tortilla on top. Bake in oven at 350 degrees until tortilla edges turn light brown, approximately 10 minutes. Repeat to make 2 more quesadillas. Top with salsa and sour cream. Serve with rice and vegetable to round out the meal. Serves 4-6.

A good resource for more frugal recipes is the book "Miserly Meals" by Joni McCoy, 2002, Bethany House Publishers. See http://www.betterbudgeting.com/frugalrecipelist.htm for other tasty recipes.

Fridgedly Frugal

Freeze-Ahead Cooking: One of the best ways to ensure that you have home cooked meals available for your family, even with a hectic schedule, is to cook and freeze meals ahead of time. There are various ways to freeze ahead and each requires varying degrees of planning and bulk cooking.

OAMC: Once-a month cooking (OAMC) involves preparing a full month's worth of dinners in a marathon weekend session. With OAMC cooking, you plan your menus for the month ahead of time, gather the ingredients and cook enough meals to feed your family for many weeks. The benefit is that you make your dinners for the entire month at one time and you do not have to make main dishes every night. The biggest downside of OAMC is that it takes up a good portion of an entire weekend to prepare a month's worth of meals. It also requires excellent planning skills as well as a lot of freezer space. Also, keep in mind that some of your family's favorite meals may not freeze well.

OAWC: With once-a-week cooking (OAWC), you choose one night per week to make 7 batches of the same meal at once. You serve one batch and freeze the rest. In four weeks you will have almost a month's worth of meals in the freezer. The benefit is that you spend less time in the kitchen during each cooking session than with once-a-month cooking. The negatives are that you have a mini-session every week and, when starting, it takes several weeks to build a variety of meals. Both methods work well as long as you have the freezer space to hold all the meals.

Some families choose to make double or triple batches each time they make a dinner that freezes well. They eat one batch that evening and freeze the other batches. This allows the cooking session to be shorter and, after a month, you will have a number of frozen meals available to choose from each week. This method works well for those who do not wish to cook in time-consuming sessions and for those who do not want to eat a meal that has been frozen nearly every night. If you have limited freezer space, this may be a good option for you as well.

Freezing ahead isn't just for dinner foods. Consider making multiple batches and freezing your favorite breakfast foods, including homemade pancakes, french toast, breakfast casseroles, muffins, breakfast breads and breakfast burritos with eggs, cheese and your favorite meat or vegetables. When it is time to reheat these foods, use the microwave, toaster or oven, just as if you were reheating a frozen brand name item from your local grocery store.

Egg and Cheese Breakfast Sandwiches

12 English muffins
1 dozen eggs
12 slices cheese, cheddar or American

Scramble eggs in large skillet. Separate muffin halves. Place an equal amount of egg on 12 muffin halves. Place a piece of sliced cheese on the egg and top with remaining muffin halves. Cool sandwiches in refrigerator. Once cooled, wrap each sandwich in a microwave safe paper towel, place them in zip-top freezer bags (several sandwiches should fit in each bag) and freeze. To heat, microwave a single sandwich wrapped in paper towel on high for one to two minutes, until cheese is melted.

You can also freeze many dessert items and simply remove them from the freezer an hour or so before needed. Brownies, cookies and cakes all freeze well. They will thaw quickly if frozen in individual pieces.

If you are new to freeze-ahead cooking, start slowly by doubling or tripling one or two freezable meals a week. In no time at all you will have many homemade frozen meals to choose from when planning your weekly menu. I recommend the book "Frozen Assets: How to Cook for a Day and Eat For a Month" by Deborah Taylor-Hough, 1999, Champion Press. The book offers excellent tips and recipes for freeze-ahead cooking. Another good resource for freezer meals is http://busycooks.about.com/od/makeaheadrecipes/.

Stock Your Pantry

Having a well-stocked pantry allows you to prepare a healthy meal at any time. Another very important reason to keep a stocked pantry is that in times of short-term financial difficulty, you can eat primarily from your stocked pantry and use your grocery money for unplanned expenses.

Keep in mind that a pantry isn't just the dry goods on the shelf.   A pantry, for our purposes, includes the items available for use in the freezer and refrigerator as well. Stocking a pantry takes some time, but over a period of a few months you should be able to make a meal at any time from your pantry, if needed.   Depending on the needs and tastes of your family, every household's pantry looks different.   Begin by looking over the Pantry List that follows.

Baking	Rice	Mild cheese
All-purpose flour	Dried potatoes	Milk
Baking soda		Sharp cheese
Baking powder	**Freezer**	Sour cream
Brown sugar	Vegetables	Yogurt
Cornstarch	Meat	
Nuts	Breads and rolls	**Seasonings**
Sugar	Frozen meals	Basil
Vanilla extract		Bay leaves
	Fruits and Veggies	Black pepper
Canned Goods	Apples	Cayenne pepper
Beans	Bananas	Chili pepper
Canned peas	Potatoes	Cinnamon, ground
Canned fruit	Onions	Garlic powder
Canned tomatoes	Garlic	Ginger, ground
Pasta sauce	Lettuce	Unsalted seasoning
Tomato sauce	Cucumbers	Nutmeg, ground
Tuna	Tomatoes	Oregano
	Carrots	Parsley
Condiments		Red pepper flakes
Honey	**Non-Food**	Rosemary
Jam or jelly	Aluminum foil	Sage, ground
Ketchup	Plastic wrap	Salt
Mayonnaise	Plastic zipper bags	Thyme
Mustard		
Parmesan	**Oils**	**Snacks**
Salad dressings	Canola oil	Crackers
Salsa	Olive oil	Popcorn
Soy sauce	Non-fat cooking spray	Pretzels
		Tortilla chips
Dry Goods	**Refrigerator**	
Cereal	Butter or margarine	**Vinegars**
Pasta	Cream cheese	Balsamic vinegar
	Eggs	Red wine vinegar

Decide which items you do not use and cross them off. Add items that your family uses which are not included. Now you have a Pantry List that you can use as a guide as you develop your well-stocked pantry. When you look over the sale flyers each week, add one or two pantry items that are on sale to your grocery list. Within a few months, your pantry should be much better stocked and your frugal menu options greatly increased.

Maintaining your pantry is not difficult. Keep at least 2 of each item you use—one that is already opened and one backup. When you open the backup, put that item on your grocery list for the next week or two when it goes on sale and you have a coupon. Put all newly purchased items in the back, so the older product is consumed first and does not expire. Ideally, you will have more than two of any item that stores for a long period of time. When you can buy an item from your pantry list at a deep discount, especially one that you use often, buy as many as you have room for as long as the items will not expire before you can use them.

If you are thinking that you just don't have enough room for a well-stocked pantry, take a good look around. You can probably find space in closets, under beds, in corners of kitchen cabinets and all around the house. You don't have to give up your bathtub, but it is worth the effort to find the space needed to support your pantry items. An extra cabinet in the laundry room might be all the extra space you need.

It is important that you know the shelf life of the products in your pantry, freezer and fridge so you use those products safely before they expire. See the USDA "Basics for Handling Food Safely" at the following USDA website: http://www.fsis.usda.gov/Fact_Sheets/Basics_for_Handling_Food_Safely/index.asp for information on food safety and storage.

Backyard Garden

One of the best ways to cut produce costs is to grow your own vegetables and fruits. Produce from your own garden tastes delicious and reduces your food bill. Growing a garden is also a wonderful learning experience for children. We began growing our own produce garden ten years ago and, to this day, my favorite thing to eat is a tomato and cucumber sandwich with vegetables fresh from the garden. I start daydreaming about them in mid-winter and, by July, when we are harvesting fresh vegetables, my dreams come true! Following are some tips to get you started with your own garden.

Don't get in over your head: There is nothing like planting your first garden only to find out you planted more than you can handle. You will become frustrated, tired and overwhelmed and give up forever. Start with a comfortable 10' X 10' area and remember that next year you can increase the size if you wish.

Location is key: Find a space for your garden that receives plenty of sun. Prep the soil by tilling it with a borrowed or rented tiller. Mixing grass in with soil adds organic material. You will need to determine what soil type you have so you know what soil amendments (topsoil, gypsum, lime, fertilizer, organic material) to add. Bring a sample of your soil to your local agricultural extension office to receive a pH and soil analysis. If you only have a small area, consider container gardening. Many varieties of different vegetables grow well in large pots.

Planting time: Once your soil is tilled and in good shape, it is time to plant. There are many types of seeds that you can start growing indoors in small containers approximately 8 weeks before replanting into the outdoor garden. You can also buy transplants of many of the popular vegetables and fruits. These little plants work beautifully, are inexpensive, and are good for the beginning gardener who may only want one plant for each type of vegetable. Good starter crops include tomatoes, beans, peas, zucchini, summer squash and cucumbers. Make sure you plant after the last expected frost. You can find out about frost information by speaking with your extension office.

How does your garden grow?: Once you have planted, you should put down a layer of newspaper and then a layer of hay straw. This will keep weeds from growing too rapidly. If you see weeds emerge, get rid of them right away. Plant the seeds or transplants far enough apart, keep them weeded and fertilize regularly and you will cut down on pest issues. Seed packs and transplant labels will indicate how far apart you need to plant the seeds or plants.

You can also put up a short wire mesh gate around your garden to discourage children, rabbits and other creatures that may rummage through your hard work. When dealing with insects, you can choose an organic route, which we have done most years, or use an insecticide from your local garden supply store. For information on which route is best, see the extension office once again. They can tell you what types of pests are most common in your area and how to best prevent them. You will also want to know what critters are good to have around because they eat the pests that can destroy your beloved garden.

Enjoy the fruits of your labor: Pick your produce when it is ripe and don't overcook your vegetables. Enjoy your wonderful produce all winter by freezing or canning, as well.

Share the bounty: You will find that as your plants begin to bear fruit, you may harvest more than you and your family can possibly eat. A sure way to endear yourself to all your friends, family and the new neighbor two doors down is through garden fresh veggies. Nothing says friendship like a homegrown tomato!

If you are hesitant about produce gardening, begin with one container plant. Find a variety that is suitable for containers and get your feet wet with a single vegetable. We have grown tomatoes (especially cherry tomatoes) successfully in containers and once you bite into that first juicy tomato, you will probably be ready to go tiller shopping!

Growing an herb garden is another easy way to add fresh and frugal flavor to your meals. If you have children, herbs are a good introduction to gardening because the plants are smaller than most vegetable and fruit plants.

For much more information on all aspects of gardening, check with your local library for books on growing vegetables, consult your agricultural extension office and speak with other people who garden in your climate. Ask them what works well for them and what problems they have encountered.

Restaurants and Take Out

As a general rule, dining out at restaurants and fast food places isn't very frugal. In addition, you probably don't want your children to grow up thinking that fast food fare is acceptable on a regular basis. But there are special occasions when you will be eating out and, for those times, there are frugal tips to consider. Following are ways to reduce your dining expenses while still enjoying the luxury of eating out.

Early Bird Specials

Many restaurants offer specials that are valid during the times when the volume of diners is lower. Usually this is before traditionally busy hours for the restaurant. For dinner meals this is around 4:30 to 6:00 p.m. Check with your favorite restaurants to see if they offer early bird specials.

Coupons

Many restaurants issue coupons for dollars off or BOGO (buy one get one free) meals. These coupons offer an opportunity to eat at good restaurants for as little as half the cost. Look for restaurant coupons in the coupon mailers that are delivered to your mailbox or in local newspapers. Consider purchasing the Entertainment Book (http://www.entertainment.com/) for your town. The Entertainment Books contain many restaurant coupons, as well as entertainment and other coupons. If you split the cost with a neighbor, friend or relative and share the coupons, you can find some very good deals. Often, Chamber of Commerce centers offer pamphlets with coupons to encourage tourists to eat out at local restaurants. Call them to see if you can get coupons when you are traveling to another city or call your local Chamber and see if they are offering any packets for your area. Restaurant.com (http://www.restaurant.com) offers a number of restaurant gift certificates at half price. Usually the gift certificate is for $25 off of the total price of the meal and the certificate costs you only $12.50. There are minimum purchase requirements on some gift certificates, so read the certificate details very carefully.

Share, Share, Share

As we all know, many restaurants give you more food than you should consume at one sitting. Why not split the appetizer or dessert (or both!) to save an extra $5 to $10. You can also take home a doggie bag, which is a completely acceptable and common practice these days. At the restaurants that offer unlimited salad and bread before the meal, you can fill up on those items and only eat a small portion of your main course. Then you can take the leftovers home and have another meal to enjoy for lunch or dinner the next day.

Family Dining

Most restaurants offer kids' meals at a fraction of the cost of adult meals. Other restaurants offer "kids nights" where children eat free with the purchase of an adult meal. Those are both good options when it is time to treat the whole family for a night on the town. Two younger children can often split an adult-sized meal or they can get an extra plate and share your meal. Nearly every restaurant offers reduced-price kids' menus, making it a little more affordable to eat out.

Auctions

A number of online auction sites have restaurant gift certificates up for bid. Often you can purchase these gift cards for 25% to 50% off the value of the card. For instance, if the gift card is worth $20, the winning bid may be $10. That is a 50% savings. If you use a coupon for your meal in addition to the gift certificate, you can get an even greater deal! Check out restaurant gift certificates on http://www.ebay.com and you will be surprised at the number of choices up for auction.

Frequent Diner Cards

Some restaurants offer frequent diner cards that give you a discount or free item after you eat there a certain number of times. There are a number of sub sandwich restaurants that offer these types of rewards. Check with your favorite places to eat to see if they offer a frequent diner benefit.

Treats for Grades and Birthdays

Many restaurants offer rewards for good grades and freebies on birthdays. Ask around at the places you eat to see if they celebrate good grades and birthdays with free food.

Eat Like a Kid Again!
In many places, you can order off the kids' menu and pay a lot less for a tasty meal that usually offers plenty of food for a lunch or light dinner.

Senior Discounts
Many restaurants offer discounts of 5% or more off the price of your meal if you are 60 years old or over. Simply asking if a senior discount is available could save you a little extra each time you eat out. If you can combine a senior discount with a frequent diner card and a gift certificate or coupon, you will really be getting some excellent deals!

Do Lunch
Sherri Allen, editor of an informational and fun family Web site at http://www.sherriallen.com offers the idea to "do lunch." She says, "Who says special meals have to be eaten in the evening? Go out for lunch instead of dinner. Most restaurants have a lunch menu that offers smaller portions of your favorite choices, as well as special lunch-only meals, for reduced prices."

Key Points To Remember

- Meal planning allows you to reduce both the cost of meals and the stress associated with wondering what to make each night when you get home from a busy day.

- Master Meal Lists and Weekly Menus will guide you in deciding what to serve each week and take the guesswork out of feeding your household.

- Freeze-ahead cooking allows you to have healthy and frugal meals ready to eat throughout the week.

- A stocked pantry reduces the stress surrounding meal planning. If you have a variety of available ingredients you will have many meal options.

- Consider growing a garden, even a small one, to reap the benefits of less expensive and wonderful tasting produce.

Key Actions To Take

- Create a Master Meal List of all the meals your family will eat. Place the list in a three-ring binder for easy reference and amend it to add new choices.

- Create a weekly menu utilizing items from your pantry and sale items from the grocery store.

- Begin freeze-ahead cooking in small doses. When you cook a freezable meal, double or triple the batch. Eat one batch that evening and freeze the other two to save for other nights.

- Stock your pantry with suggested kitchen essentials purchased on sale.

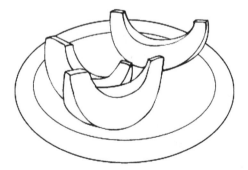

Chapter 4

Frugal Fun

Celebrations, Holidays and Gift Giving

Celebrations provide wonderful opportunities to enjoy happy occasions surrounded by friends and family. They bring people together in environments that often involve lots of food and gifts, as well. Although the company at your celebration may be "priceless," there is always a cost to the festivities. Let's look at some ways to cut expenses when you are celebrating birthdays, hosting parties, and enjoying the holidays.

Frugal Parties

- Pick a theme such as Game Night, Movie Night, Football Night or Potluck Night. Offer snacks based on the theme and use inexpensive entertainment, such as a movie, football game or board games.

- Buy deeply discounted paper goods in solid colors after the various holidays and save them until you need them. Party stores often sell paper products with generic party designs for 50 cents a package versus $2 for a name brand.

- Use candles, purchased on clearance of course, to create an elegant or romantic mood. January after-holiday sales are where you will find the best deals on candles.

- Use flowers from your garden as a centerpiece. If you have to buy flowers, only purchase those in season. Vegetables, fruit or nuts, in a crystal bowl, make a lovely centerpiece.

- When feeding a large group, have a potluck dinner or prepare a big piece of meat (like a turkey) and have everyone else bring the sides, such as pasta salad, vegetables, salad, bread and dessert.

- Host a wine or beer tasting party and have the guests bring their favorite bottles of wine or micro-brewed beer to share. You provide a light meal or appetizers and your guests can bring their favorite drinks.

Frugal Children's Birthday Parties

- The most frugal place to hold your child's birthday party is at home. If weather permits, have it outdoors with activities such as a scavenger hunt, water balloon toss, sack races or beanbag toss. The beanbag toss and scavenger hunt can easily be held indoors, as well.

- Have the party in the park. You can usually reserve a gazebo or covered picnic area at no charge and there is plenty to do at most parks. Offer games, cake, drinks and a goody bag. If the party is during mealtime include, hot dogs, chips and a veggie tray or watermelon slices. Cleanup is easy and everyone gets to enjoy time outside together.

- Bake the cake yourself or use cupcakes and let the kids decorate them as part of the party activities.

- Print the invitations on your computer or make them by hand on thick paper with your child.

- Use white lunch sacks and have the kids decorate them as the party favor bags. You could have them decorate crowns if the theme is princess/prince.

- Buy party favors at the dollar store or on clearance after holidays. Stock up throughout the year.
- Have a sleepover with a movie-night theme. For instance, let the birthday child choose two action movies, provide popcorn and let them stay up late.

The Holidays

- If your family/friends agree on a gift giving budget or method, everyone's holidays will be less financially draining. Although it may seem awkward to bring up the subject, ask relatives to agree to stay within a set budget. This can make the entire gift giving adventure more fun and easier to live with in January, when the bills usually start showing up.

- If your whole family agrees, choose names, with each person responsible for buying a gift for only one other person. If you set a maximum dollar amount, it will keep costs down even more and ensure the gift exchange is fair for everyone. Capping the gift cost at $15 to $20 is a good rule of thumb. This method of gift exchange is especially frugal when very large families get together. Everyone will still take home a gift but costs will be contained.

- Another sure way to decrease costs is to buy gifts only for the children. How many times have you received a gift from a distant relative that wasn't exactly something you would use? Save your relatives some time, trouble (what in the world should I get for my second cousin who I haven't seen in five years?), and money and only purchase presents for the little ones.

- Hit garage sales for holiday decorations. Great décor can be purchased at yard sales for a fraction of the retail cost.

- Use natural items like pinecones or a large bowl of fruit for decoration.

- Decorate with clearance items from the previous year's holiday sales, such as using colored glass ball ornaments in a nice crystal bowl as a centerpiece.

- Agreeing to exchange homemade gifts is a thoughtful and frugal way to give during the holidays. Examples of homemade gifts include baked goods, homemade mixes for various foods, knitted scarves, themed scrapbooks, ornaments, coupon books and homemade cookbooks.

Gift Giving Throughout the Year

Have you ever experienced the holiday letdown that occurs in January when all the celebrations are over, the gifts have been given and your credit card debt has hit a new high? Planning your gift giving for the year will allow you to include the annual estimated amount (divided by 12) in your monthly budgets so that gift time doesn't involve going into debt. Remember to include the gifts you give for birthdays, holidays, anniversaries and all other celebrations your family enjoys.

 Make a list at the beginning of the year with the names of people for whom you will be buying gifts. Throughout the year, you can purchase gifts for those on your list when items are on sale, instead of going to the store at the last minute to buy a full-price item for someone. Establish an area in your house for storing the gift items and, when it comes time to give, you will have plenty of wonderful and frugal choices. That may mean buying for a May birthday in January or doing your holiday kid's shopping at a June toy clearance. A smart shopper looks for gifts throughout the year at many different types of locations.

Following are some tips for finding and giving great gifts at smart prices.

- Shop the after-holiday sales as soon as the items are marked down 50% or more. Call your favorite stores to get the markdown schedule. Buy during these sales to save on gift wrap, bows, boxes and decorations. You will often find nice gifts to give people throughout the year, including candles and decorative glass bowls.

- Don't think that holiday clearance sales only have holiday items for sale. Baskets can be used for making lovely gifts filled with all sorts of wonderful presents. You can also break up clearance gift boxes that contain food and non-perishable items. Eat the food or gift it and then save the non-perishable plates, cheese board and knife for a gift basket to give later. Save the solid red Christmas clearance items, including plates, napkins and candy, for Valentine's Day decorating and celebrations. Use the green clearance items for St Patty's Day parties. Save the Valentine's Day red paper items, purchased at clearance prices, to use during Fourth of July festivities.

- Find clothing gifts at seasonal sales when stores are clearing out the end of season items to make room for new stock. Many national department stores mark large selections of clothes and seasonal gifts down 75% and more when a season ends. This is the time to stock up on gifts and clothes for the whole next year. Start looking for the winter clearance sales starting in late January and the summer clearance in August. Don't just limit yourself to brick and mortar stores—on-line clearance sales are equally as fabulous!

- Gifts from the kitchen are always loved and often very frugal. Cookies, sweet breads, fudge, jams and jellies, and other canned items all make great gifts for anytime of year. Simply use a basket (from a previous gift you received, yard sale or clearance sale) or a gift bag (bought at holiday clearance for 75% to 90% off) to present the yummy gift. The gift will probably cost much less than a store-bought item and the person who gets to enjoy your delicious creations will be thrilled with your thoughtfulness!

• Gift baskets are a creative and fun way to give a custom gift. You can make a gift basket for any occasion and fill it slowly with items you find at great prices. You can start a basket months in advance to make sure you have plenty of items to wow the person on the receiving end. A movie themed basket might include popcorn, candy, soda, a recently released or classic DVD, and gift certificates to a movie theater or rental store.

• Give personalized gift certificates for services that friends and family may need. A new mom may love the gift of babysitting. A special dinner made and delivered would please anyone who doesn't always have the time to cook. Someone who needs help around the house would love a coupon book for mowing the lawn, cleaning out the attic and washing the windows. The gift of your time is precious, always appreciated and certainly a frugal choice.

• Online auction sites are great places to locate those hard to find unique items at a reasonable cost. You can find just about anything and often the prices for auction items start very low. See http://www.ebay.com.

• Pick up gently used items, such as toys and books, for your own children at yard sales. Often you can also find new items, collectibles or antiques suitable for gift giving as well.

• Make a scrapbook for someone special with pictures collected over the year. Ask others who may have pictures to donate them for the book. You can also ask others to write short notes about events, nice memories or funny stories to include in the book.

• Regifting is an acceptable frugal gift giving option, as long as it is handled correctly. For those who don't know, regifting is the practice of taking a gift you have been given (but haven't used) and presenting it as a gift to someone else. Typically, someone regifts a present when they receive something they already have or simply won't use. For example, instead of letting an extra copy of a book go unread, a regifter will offer the book to a bookworm friend. Rather than allowing that beautiful new sweater to hang in the closet unworn because she is allergic to wool, a regifter will give it to her sister.

Etiquette experts agree that regifting is appropriate, as long as a few basic rules are followed. You should not regift a present to a close friend or family member of the person who originally gave the gift to you. Don't offer the regifted present under the guise of having searched far and wide until you found just the right thing. Only regift an item because you think the recipient will truly enjoy the item. It is appropriate to let the recipient know you are regifting to them a present you have been given. For example, you can tell a friend that you received a duplicate copy of your favorite cookbook and you thought she would enjoy it.

• There are alternatives to purchased gifts that can promote a wonderful sense of community and well being for all involved. Donate your time or resources to a charity as the person's gift. Make sure you choose a charity that is important to the person so he or she knows the gift was well thought out and personalized just for him or her. Organize a community food, toy or clothing drive and make a donation to the charity that the gift recipient chooses.

The following calendar lists items that typically go on sale during certain months. Watch your store flyers for specific product sales.

January	February	March	April
Holiday clearance for clothing, gifts, wrap, decorations, coats, gloves and hats	Valentine's Day, Presidents Day clearance, winter boots, gloves and hats	Winter clothing clearance	Spring dress clearance late in April, rain boots, raincoats, Easter clearance
May Mother's Day and Memorial Day specials and clearance	**June** Father's Day specials and clearance, men's clothing, bathing suits	**July** July Fourth specials and clearance, summer wear sales	**August** Back-to-school specials and summer clothing clearance, summer toy clearance
September Labor Day specials, more back-to-school clearance, summer clothing clearance, fall clothing sales	**October** Fall and winter clothing sales, candy sales	**November** Halloween clearance, Fall décor and Thanksgiving sales, Election Day and Veterans Day sales	**December** Holiday sales, Thanksgiving and Fall décor clearance. Holiday clearance begins Dec. 26, every year!

Affordable Family Fun

Entertainment and family fun do not have to cost you every bit of extra income that you have. Because the question of what to do and where to go never seems to end when you have children, it's important to find affordable entertainment options so you don't break your budget. The great news is that there are plenty of low and no cost adventures for your whole family. Following are 26 ideas for affordable family fun that kids of every age can enjoy.

1. Find out the schedule for free days at local museums and spend the afternoon discovering dinosaur fossils and 16th Century paintings.

2. Call the local theater and ask about preview/rehearsal dates for plays. You can often see a play at a greatly reduced price during the preview rehearsals.

3. Try minor league sporting events that usually cost much less than major league sporting games.

4. Memberships to zoos, museums and science centers are often well worth the initial investment if you frequent the locations.

5. Concerts in the park are often free on evenings and weekends. If you pack your lunch or dinner (vs. stopping to buy take-out) the outing will be that much more affordable.

6. Many businesses, such as grocery stores, newspapers, TV or radio stations, manufacturing plants, train stations and airports, will offer tours and field trips for your family. Although most adults might not view a trip to the grocery store as family fun, children love to learn about the world around them and field trips are an ideal teaching opportunity. Simply call ahead to see if any businesses offer this service in your area.

7. Farm visits are a great way to show children where their food comes from. Visit a local farmer's market and ask some of the vendors if they have open house events or offer tours.

8. A day trip to the beach (if you live near the coast) is a wonderful way to experience the ocean. Collecting seashells, walking along the shore and building sand castles are inexpensive ways to enjoy nature. Avoid

high beach prices by packing your lunch and plenty to drink.

9. Pull out the board games a few times a month. Not only is this less expensive than renting a movie or going out to eat, it is a wonderful way to spend time with your family and friends in the comfort of your own home.

10. Head to your local library for children's reading time. It's free and fun! After reading time is over you can stay and check out a few books to take home and read for the next couple of weeks at no cost.

11. Many national bookstore chains also offer free children's reading time. Call around your area to see when the reading days and times are in your town.

12. There are a number of national movie chains that offer free or reduced morning movies during the summer. This is a great way to get out of the house on a hot day and enjoy watching a movie in a theater.

13. Check out your local parks and recreation departments. They offer inexpensive arts and crafts, cooking and dance classes, as well as many other low cost ways to learn new skills.

14. Go bowling. Many bowling alleys will issue coupons for free games in the local paper. You will still need to rent shoes, but the cost is minimal.

15. Make your own bowling game using 2-liter plastic soda bottles. Leave them empty for the younger children and fill them with sand for the older ones. Use an appropriate weight ball based on the child's age and the weight of the bottles. You can use your driveway, basement, garage or living room and play as long as you like at no cost. Another benefit: no special shoes required.

16. Grow your own fun by planting a garden with your family. Not only will your children have a great time,

they will also learn the value of growing their own food when they get to harvest and enjoy it!

17. Scrapbooking is a wonderful way to spend time while getting all your photos out of boxes and into albums. Albums can be made using very old family photos, pictures of the kids when they were younger, or recent photos of the family trip or holiday party.

18. Head to the park with a picnic and spend the day swinging, bike riding, kite flying, walking the trails, playing ball and eating your frugally packed lunch and snacks. Everyone will sleep well that night and your wallet will be pretty happy, too.

19. Free festivals are lots of fun and usually offer free entertainment. Pack a few snacks and cold drinks and enjoy looking at all the arts and crafts booths and listening to the music. You may even find a frugal and beautiful gift for someone on your gift list.

20. Have a scavenger hunt either in the house or outside. Make a list of 10 items for the kids to find and watch them go. If the kids are too young to read, draw pictures of the items they need to find or just tell them what to look for, one item at a time.

21. Enjoy your own neighborhood by going on nature walks, riding bikes, and chatting with your neighbors along the way.

22. Rainy day? Have an indoor picnic by moving the coffee table out of the way, spreading out the picnic blanket, having lunch on the floor and making smores for dessert (it's not necessary to heat the marshmallows).

23. Enjoy music time by singing songs, playing instruments, and marching around the house with your "band." It may be loud, but it is so much fun! If you are short on musical instruments, grab a pot and a wooden spoon and drum away.

24. Many home improvement centers offer free workshops for children on the weekends. The children and the parents learn firsthand how to make birdhouses, picture frames and many other creative projects. Usually the store pays for all the supplies and the children take home the projects they make.

25. Bake cookies or brownies and then surprise your neighbor or teacher. Putting a smile on someone else's face is always great fun.

26. Take part in volunteer activities through religious or other organizations to help those in your community. Volunteer opportunities exist all over town, including at nursing homes, animal shelters, schools and children's hospitals.   Often local newspapers list available volunteer opportunities in the community.

Travel Near and Far

Ever feel like you really need a vacation but don't think you can afford one? If so, keep reading to learn how you can travel inexpensively and still enjoy a fantastic trip. Remember, the key is to spend quality time, not your whole bank account, on your vacation. Following are tips for frugal travel, both far away and just around the corner.

Travel to Far Away Places
Frugal travel is not limited to tents and campfires in order to get out and see the world, although that is a great frugal option! There are wonderful bargains available for just about any location you would like to visit. The key to the greatest savings is flexibility and patience. If you can wait for a good deal and are flexible on arrival and departure dates and times, you will get the best rates.

If you aren't checking travel rates online, you are missing out on some of the best deals. There are many Web sites available that offer very low airfares to places around the world. They all have different rules, so read carefully when buying tickets. You will also need access to a printer to print out the hard copies of your tickets. Take a look at Travelocity.com at http://www.travelocity.com and Clark Howard's Web site at http://www.clarkhoward.com. Each site offers a wealth of travel information, including many excellent deals on airfare, car rentals and other travel related expenses.

Membership in frequent flyer programs is a terrific way to earn free round-trip tickets. You can earn miles by flying a particular airline and/or by using a credit card that issues frequent flyer miles for purchases you make. Some programs offer miles for long-distance phone minutes, as well.

Warehouse clubs are now in the travel business and offer some competitive prices, especially on some of the packages that include a car and hotel room. If you are a member of a warehouse club, take a look at their prices when gathering your quotes for a trip.

When booking hotels, there are many ways to reduce costs:

- Call the local hotel number (not the toll-free number) and ask for their best rate. Often the customer service person at the hotel will be able to offer a better rate than the customer service person who answers the national phone number for the hotel chain.

- Ask about corporate rates (even if you are self employed).

- Ask for AAA or senior discounts.

- Negotiate with the manager. This works best if it is off-season or the hotel is only half full for the evening.

- Hostels and college dorm rooms are interesting and frugal places to stay when visiting locations throughout the world. For information on hostels, including prices and hostel locations, see http://www.hostels.com.

- Stay in a hotel room with a kitchen and prepare many of your meals for much less money than restaurant meals. Purchase breakfast and sandwich items from a grocery store and only eat out once a day while traveling.

- Use a credit card that gives you hotel points for using the card. When you stay at a qualifying hotel, you can redeem the points for free nights in hotels around the world. Of course, only use a credit card if you can pay it off, in full, each month.

Heading Out for a Few Days
Day and weekend trips are great ways to travel with the family, stay within your budget and still enjoy a fun vacation. Short trips to areas within driving distance of your home can allow you a great deal of flexibility while keeping you within your budget. Consider some of the following options the next time you are planning a trip.

Tent or cabin camping: Enjoy the great outdoors, bring your own frugal meals, see your state and surrounding states, and show your children the beauty of nature. Look into camping options at state parks, national parks, national forests and private campgrounds. Activities that some parks and campgrounds offer include hiking, fishing, canoeing, swimming, biking, horseback riding and more. Some of my most wonderful vacation memories are of camping with my family in different parts of the country in an RV (recreational vehicle). Consider renting an RV and staying at campgrounds. You will have comfortable beds and air-conditioning and you will still be able to enjoy all the sights and sounds of nature.

Travel off-peak: Some of the best deals can be found when business at popular destinations is slow. Beaches, mountain resorts, ski lodges and other locations offer great rates during off-peak months, when the tourists are not flocking to their areas. Consider visiting just before the season begins or just after it ends to get lower rates and still be able to enjoy the amenities. Hotels in many larger cities and near airports often offer reduced rates during the weekend when business travelers have gone home for the weekend.

Call direct: When booking a hotel, remember to call the local number for the hotel, not the 1-800 national number, to get the best rates, especially when the hotel is not fully booked. Remember that the closer the hotel is to a popular destination, such as the beach, the more expensive it will be. If you stay at a hotel room right on the beach you will pay much more than if you book a room in a hotel three blocks from the beach. When staying at a hotel, look for one with a reasonable rate and free breakfast. That's one less meal to prepare or purchase.

House and condo rentals: If you plan on staying at a location for a week or more, consider renting a house or condominium. There are many good deals to be found during the off-season. Do a web search for vacation rentals in the town you would like to visit to find rates and available rentals.

Visit family and friends: Visiting family in other towns and states is a good way to keep everyone connected and visit new places. An overnight stay with relatives saves you money that can be spent enjoying aquariums, zoos and other places your family would enjoy.

Meals on a trip: Pack snacks that travel well, such as pretzels, cheese, cut up veggies and mini-muffins. Don't forget drinks because the sodas at gas stations are much more expensive than the drinks you bought on sale with a coupon. If you are eating out, go to restaurants during lunch instead of dinner. Food on a dinner menu is often much higher priced than the same food on the lunch menu. Have a picnic in the park for dinner instead of eating at the more expensive restaurant.

Key Points to Remember

• Parties and celebrations are opportunities to gather together and have fun, not foil your monthly budget.

• With some creativity, your less expensive party can be just as enjoyable as a more costly event. The biggest difference will be you won't be stuck with a huge bill to pay once a frugal party has ended.

• Remember that children's parties do not have to equal the cost and extravagance of most weddings! A simple party with fun activities is the responsible and frugal road to take.

• If your family agrees to stay within a set budget for gift giving, you will all enjoy the holidays more without the stress of overspending.

• Plan your gift giving for the year. Start a gift closet or drawer and you will always have frugal items to give.

• There are many affordable family activities to enjoy year round, such as museums, plays and outings to the library.

• Consider checking costs for flights, car rentals and hotels using online resources. You may be able to find a much better rate than through more traditional travel resources.

• Enjoying day and weekend trips is a wonderful way to see your state without having to pay for airline tickets or a full week in a hotel.

• There are a number of fun day trips you can take that won't involve an overnight stay, but will allow you an opportunity to get away for a few hours and enjoy your area.

Key Actions To Take

- Start a Gift List including those people you know you will be giving gifts to during the year.

- Start a gift closet and begin to fill it with frugally purchased items you can use for those on your list.

- Approach your family about a spending budget or restriction of some kind for the holidays, if you do not already have one in place.

- Plan a day or evening adventure and choose a frugal option, such as a hike, picnic in the park, trip to the museum or neighborhood potluck.

- The next time you need to fly, rent a car, or rent a hotel room, visit Clark Howard's Web site at http://www.clarkhoward.com and Travelocity at http://www.travelocity.com for information on the best current rates. Use that information to book online or call the airline, car rental facility or hotel directly to negotiate a better rate using the online quote.

Chapter 5

Take Care Of Yourself

We all want to look and feel good without exceeding our budgets. Can it be done? Absolutely. There are many ways to reduce clothing, medical and fitness costs that don't involve sending your budget to the emergency room!

Dress Your Best For a Whole Lot Less

The cost of clothing can leave your budget in need of serious mending if you aren't a smart spender. Making the most of your clothing allowance is much easier when you pay attention to the sales cycles of the stores. Shopping the seasonal clearance sales will help you maintain a complete wardrobe without ever paying full price for clothes again. You will also realize the greatest value when you buy clothes that are versatile. Every piece of clothing you purchase should be appropriate for more than one type of occasion and mix and match with at least two items in your existing wardrobe.

The stores at which you choose to shop significantly influence the price you pay for clothes. If you shop around, you will see there are good clothing deals to be found at many different stores and it helps to know what each type of store has to offer.

Department Stores: You will typically pay more for clothing at a department store than any other store discussed, but if you require a higher-priced line of clothing, you can still find bargains. There are good buys to be found at department stores when you shop the sales and use coupons. Buy your clothes during the seasonal clearance specials, where you can often find brand name items discounted 50% to 75%. Use the coupons from your newspaper or sales flyer to save even more. If you have a store credit card, check your bill for the coupons that are often enclosed.

Discount Clothing Chains: You will generally find better deals at discount clothing chains than at the pricier department stores. There is always a good selection of lower-priced brand and off-brand clothing. Discount stores are absolutely the place to be when they have clearance sales! Stock up during seasonal clearance and you will be ready for next year.

Mass Merchandisers: Don't forget about mass merchandisers, such as the super mart stores. You can find great bargains on casual clothing and accessories in the clearance racks. Be sure to check the endcaps (at the end of the aisles) for even more savings. Often the best deals are not easily seen. The key with mass merchandisers is to check the clearance endcaps and racks on a regular basis, as they are always marking down additional items.

Outlet Stores: Outlet stores can be the source of real bargains, but you need to be careful. Just because a store is in an outlet mall does not mean that it offers good buys. When shopping at outlets, look around at all the stores that interest you before you buy. If you are shopping for a specific item, do some comparison shopping at other retail stores, both online and B&M (brick and mortar stores), before heading to the outlets, so you know what a good price on the item would be. Often, outlet malls offer coupon books loaded with coupons for the stores in the mall. Check with the outlet mall office about any promotions or coupons.

Warehouse Clubs: Surprisingly, warehouse clubs often offer some good deals on clothing and accessories. Be aware that the stock changes frequently and that the same merchandise may not be available from trip to trip. If you keep your eyes open, you may find real bargains at these stores.

Thrift Stores: Consignment and thrift stores offer some very good deals on gently worn items. Shopping at thrift stores near affluent neighborhoods will offer a larger selection of more expensive name brand items. You may have to look through many racks to find a piece you like, but if you are up to the challenge of thrift store shopping, you may be pleasantly surprised.

Yard Sales: Another frugal way to dress your family and find all sorts of other treasures is by shopping at yard sales. Yard sales (also known as garage sales, rummage sales and tag sales) offer an array of used, and sometimes new, merchandise. Since the used items can range from barely used to worn out past their useful lives, it's important to inspect anything you might buy to make sure it is in good shape. You certainly don't want to purchase something just to have it fall apart in a few weeks!

To find yard sales in your area, check in the classified ad section of your local newspaper. Not everyone runs ads for their yard sales, so be sure to keep your eyes open for the yard sale signs that are typically posted at intersections, on street signs, on telephone poles, at neighborhood entrances and in front of people's homes on Saturday mornings. Most yard sales are held on Saturdays, although some areas hold sales on Fridays as well.

If there are several advertised yard sales you want to visit, map out your route. Start early and bring snacks, drinks and a good dose of patience. You may go to three or four sales before you find anything you want to buy. Also, be sure to bring cash, because credit cards and checks are generally not accepted. When you do unearth a good deal and are ready to make a purchase, don't be afraid to negotiate with the seller. It is common practice and most sellers are happy to take less for an item if it means they can get rid of it.

Online Shopping: Shopping online is a great way to find the items you need while avoiding the challenges associated with going from store to store, such as parking and spending money on gasoline. Open 24 hours a day, online shopping allows you to browse from the comfort of your own home, in your pajamas if you choose. Online shopping also enables you to locate those hard-to-find items quickly. Weeks of checking one store after another can be replaced with just a little typing and a few clicks.

Responsible Internet shopping can save you bundles of money and time, both of which can be spent on more enjoyable activities. The key to successful and smart Internet shopping is to know when to say "no." It is far too easy to find a great outfit online, whip out your credit card and pay full price and high shipping charges. That's not a good deal if you could have bought the same outfit at the local brick and mortar location for 30% off and no shipping charges.

In order for a purchase to be a good deal on the Internet, you need to look for items that are on sale and have no shipping charges. If you are not sure if the price of an item is a good deal, compare the price to ads in the Sunday paper or the prices at other online and traditional retailers. Also, keep in mind that if an online company has a brick and mortar store located in your state, they will probably charge you sales tax. Pay close attention to the total cost of online purchases, including the cost of the items, shipping and handling charges, and taxes.

Use Internet codes (also called Internet coupons) to increase savings. Internet codes are coupon codes that can be redeemed at online retailers. Companies offer the online coupons to promote interest in their Web sites and there are exceptional bargains to be found using coupon codes. Common coupon values are $5 off a purchase of $15 or more, $10 off $35 or more, free shipping, or a "free item" with purchase. Occasionally, you will even find coupons for $10 off any $10 minimum purchase. Types of coupons include "first-time buyer discounts" or special codes to be entered in the "Gift Certificate" or "Coupon" spaces upon checkout. Online coupons can be found at a multitude of coupon sites on the Internet. One of the best sites for coupons is Freelancebyu (http://www.freelancebyu.com). Operated by Anjie Hresan-Henley, who has been featured on the Today show for her ability to discover deals and save money, Freelancebyu makes it easy to find hundreds of coupon codes in one place. To access the Internet coupons, go to the website and click on the "Shopping" link.

You may also receive coupon codes from Internet retailers when you order from them. When you make a purchase, the retailer may send you an e-mail with a code for dollars off or a percentage off your next purchase.

Making an online purchase using a coupon code is simple, usually requiring just one or two more steps than a regular online purchase. After entering the usual details, such as name, address, payment information and items you wish to purchase, you have the opportunity to enter the coupon code. Your adjusted total (the full cost minus the discount from the coupon code) should be displayed. This allows you to verify the discount was applied before you finalize the sale. The coupon codes are usually restricted to one per household and only one coupon per purchase.

Most coupon codes have expiration dates, which should be indicated on the Web site where you found the coupon. If you find a coupon code without an accompanying expiration date and are unsure if it's still valid, try it. If it's still valid, it will work. If it's no longer valid, you will see that the discount was not applied and be able to cancel the purchase before the sale is completed.

Reductions on Damaged Merchandise: Have you ever found a great shirt on sale then realized it was missing a button or had a small makeup stain? Ask for a further reduction in the price of any damaged items and usually you will receive at least another 10% off. All you have to do is ask.

Fit and Frugal

Do you think you have to spend hundreds of dollars a year on an expensive gym membership in order to stay fit? Well, you don't. There are plenty of frugal exercise alternatives that will keep your body and your bank account in good shape. Don't let cost be the reason you avoid a workout, because exercise is just too important. Exercise can improve your self-image and attitude, increase your energy, and reduce the risks of many health conditions. Remember to speak with your doctor before starting any exercise program.

Put on your walking shoes: One of the easiest ways to exercise is to walk. You can walk in your neighborhood, the park, a school track and just about anywhere else. If the weather is cold or rainy, go to your local mall and do laps for 30-45 minutes. Walk with a friend to stay motivated. Listen to music that keeps you moving quickly and you will get a great fast-paced workout.

Exercise with your children: Playing basketball, riding bikes, jumping rope, swimming and running are all excellent ways to get and stay in shape. In addition to helping yourself, when you exercise with your children you demonstrate the importance of keeping fit and help them avoid the obesity that affects so many of today's children.

Out and about workout: Whenever you leave your house, you can find ways to increase your daily amount of exercise. If you can bike, jog or walk to work you have not only exercised, but you have saved on gas as well. When you have the option to take the stairs vs. the elevator, get stepping. When you drive somewhere, park a little farther away than usual so you will have to walk a few extra paces. The key is to keep moving and not in the direction of the cookie jar!

Create your own aerobics class: You can take an aerobics, yoga or stretching class anytime you want with exercise videos or DVDs. Try out exercise videos/DVDs from your local library, video rental store or a friend's collection. If possible, review a tape before buying one to ensure you will enjoy the routine.

Shake things up: During the week, enjoy more than one type of exercise. You will keep from getting bored and you will work out different parts of your body. Fitness experts recommend exercising for at least 30 minutes every day. Again, remember to consult with your doctor before beginning any exercise program.

Curb Your Medical Expenses

We all know that medical costs are extremely high and it is important to do our best to stay healthy. We also know, however, that we can't prevent every medical issue. When something happens and you require healthcare, remember that it is up to you to be a good advocate for yourself regarding your medical costs. Health insurers are in business to make a profit. The hospitals and doctors are busy treating patients' needs while keeping an eye on their own bottom lines. You are the only one whose primary concerns are you and your money. Following are steps you can take to protect yourself from medical billing and insurance errors, as well as reduce your costs for prescription medication.

Understand your insurance coverage: It is vitally important that you understand what is (and is not) covered under your health insurance policy. If a procedure, doctor's visit, hospitalization or other service requires prior authorization, make sure you get it. Do not assume that everything is covered based on your doctor's approval. Call your insurance company yourself to verify that authorizations are granted. Identify doctors who are in-network to avoid paying additional out-of-network costs. To determine in-network doctors for your area, visit the insurance company's Web site or call the customer service number listed on your insurance card. Keep detailed notes about authorizations, treatment, and all contact with the insurance company. If there is a dispute about coverage authorization, you will need to know with whom you spoke, what was said and the dates of your conversations.

If you and your spouse have health insurance through each other's employers, make sure that the insurance companies coordinate benefits when there is a claim. The primary insurance company (usually the insurance provided by your own employer) will pay first and then the secondary insurance provider (usually your insurance provided by your spouse's employer) will pay their share of the remaining balance.

Stay on top of your medical bills: Verify that the charges on your medical bills are accurate. Overcharging is a common occurrence and unless you notify the doctor or hospital, the error will not get corrected. Errors you should look for include billing twice for the same procedure, billing for medicine that was never given, billing for equipment that was not used, billing for a longer period of time than something was actually used and billing for a lab test that was ordered but later cancelled. When you are released from the hospital, ask for an itemized bill so you can see exactly what the hospital has billed you and your insurance company.

Use a three-ring binder to organize your medical bills, EOBs (Explanation of Benefits sent by the insurance company), and detailed records of communication with your insurance company and health care providers. Include a separate section for each person in your household. It will help you immensely to have all your documentation in one place if you ever have to appeal a claim decision.

Appeal, appeal, appeal: If you plan to dispute a charge with your insurance company, be prepared! Take detailed notes regarding all contact you have had with the insurance company and the medical provider. Write down dates and times of calls, names of people you have spoken with, and details about the conversation. When an insurance company denies a medical claim, you need to contact them immediately to discuss the denial. Have all your paperwork in front of you. Remain calm and courteous. Becoming angry will not help. Often, a clerical error is detected during the first call and the claim is paid with no further difficulty.

If the claim has not been paid after your first phone call, ask the customer service representative what the procedure is for requesting a review of your claim. Usually you will need to submit the request by mail. Write a calm and informative letter indicating the reason you feel the claim should be paid. Include copies of all supporting documentation, such as medical bills and doctors' letters. If there were any special circumstances that warranted additional care above the originally authorized procedure, have your doctor document them. Send in the request immediately because many providers only give you a certain amount of time to file an appeal.

If your claim still is not approved, contact your state's Department of Insurance to seek assistance. When you call, ask if there is an ombudsman who can assist you with your denied claim. An ombudsman is a customer service agent within the Department of Insurance who works with consumers to review complaints.

Flex your medical dollars: Many employers offer medical flexible spending accounts (FSA's) that allow the employees to contribute pre-tax dollars to be used for non-reimbursed medical expenses. When the employee has an out-of-pocket medical expense, they can use the flexible spending account to pay for those expenses. Contact your Human Resources department for more information.

Lower Prescription Costs
As the price of prescription drugs increase, consumers are forced to identify ways to lessen those expenses while still taking care of themselves.

Generic Drugs: Generic prescriptions can cut the cost of brand name drugs by more than half in some cases. Let your doctor know you are trying to keep expenses down. Indicate that you prefer the generic form of a drug if it will be just as effective. Often, generic over-the-counter drugs work just as well as name brands. Ask your doctor if generics are a good option for you.

Samples: Doctors' offices receive samples from drug companies to give to their patients. Most doctors are happy to give you a sample or starter pack of these drugs. This lets you and your doctor have an opportunity to see how you react to the drug before you purchase a month's supply or more. Just ask your doctor for a sample on your next visit.

Mail Order: Some insurance companies allow members to mail order up to three months worth of a prescription for the cost of one month. This will cut your annual costs significantly! Ask your insurance company if they offer this benefit.

Prescription Transfer Incentives: Many pharmacies offer incentives if you transfer prescriptions to them (usually gift certificates from their stores). For example, you may have a coupon that states that you will receive a $10 gift certificate from ABC Drug Store with any new or transferred prescription filled at that pharmacy. You will usually have to pay for your prescription or co-pay to receive the $10 gift certificate. In areas that offer prescription incentives, you can find coupons in Sunday newspapers, weekly sale flyers and online at company Web sites. Many pharmacies will honor competitors transfer incentive coupons. Call the pharmacies in your area to see if they are offering any transfer incentives.

Bulk Buying for Over-the-Counter Drugs: Buying a larger size package of over-the-counter (OTC) medication can be a very good deal. Determine who is offering the best buys by calculating and comparing the cost-per-unit of your OTC medicines at drug stores, grocery stores and warehouse clubs.

Shop at Local Warehouse Clubs: Many warehouse club pharmacies offer prescriptions at a lower price than traditional pharmacies. Call your local warehouse clubs to compare prices.

Medicare Prescription Drug Coverage: As of January 1, 2006, Medicare prescription insurance should be available for a monthly premium. The insurance pays for approximately half of prescription expenses after a deductible is met. There are a number of eligibility requirements and plan options. Visit the Medicare Web site at http://www.medicare.gov for more information.

Partnership for Prescription Assistance: The Partnership for Prescription Assistance (PPA) is a national group consisting of pharmaceutical companies, doctors, patient advocates and pharmacists. The PPA offers access to over 475 public and private patient assistance programs designed to provide free and low cost prescriptions to those who have no prescription coverage. Once you provide the required information, you will be sent applications for the plans for which you appear to qualify. Depending on the program you choose, you will be able to pick up your medicines at your doctor's office or local pharmacy or have them mailed to you. For more information, see http://www.pparx.org or call 1-888-477-2669.

Together RX Access ™ Card: Sponsored by large, well-known pharmaceutical companies, the Together RX Access ™ Card offers discounts on prescriptions from 25% - 40% off the retail cost of name brand and prescription drugs, as well as other prescription products. The card is free and there are strict eligibility requirements. In order to qualify for the discount card, you must not be eligible for Medicare, you can not have any public or private prescription drug coverage, and you must meet income requirements. For a single person, annual income must not be more than $30,000; for a family of two, annual income must not be more than $40,000; for a family of three, $50,000; for a family of four, $60,000; and for a family of five, $70,000. If your family has six or more people, contact the plan for assistance. When using the card, you will receive your discount at the pharmacy and there are no refund forms to submit. Discount amounts depend on the individual pharmacies and their pricing structure, as well as the specific drug purchased. Go to the Web site at http://www.togetherrxaccess.com or call 1-800-444-4106 to find out more information.

Key Points To Remember

- If you pay attention to the sale cycles of your favorite clothing stores, you can buy the clothing you prefer at a greatly reduced cost. If you are flexible and willing to shop at different places for your clothing, you can save even more. Shopping online and using coupon codes can also save you bundles when dressing to look your best.

- Consider low and no-cost options for regular exercising, including walking, hiking, biking and aerobics tapes.

- Remember that when it comes to medical expenses, you are your best advocate. Stay on top of your medical bills, know what you are being charged for, understand what your insurance covers, and remember your right to appeal if you do not feel your claim is being processed correctly.

- Explore all options for lowering prescription costs, including generic drugs, samples, mail order, transfer incentives, bulk buying, warehouse clubs, and government and manufacturer programs.

Key Actions To Take

- Watch end of season sales so you can grab the jacket you have been eyeing at a fraction of the retail cost.

- Use coupon codes found on Web sites such as http://www.freelancebyu.com to save money on online purchases.

- Keep all medical bills and EOBs in a file after you look them over carefully to determine if there are any errors. Address errors immediately with the insurance company and health care provider.

- If you do not have any prescription drug coverage, contact the PPA and Together RX Access programs for more information on the services they provide.

Chapter 6

Cutting Household Costs

Keeping your home up and running is a worthy and often costly challenge. Thankfully, there are ways to lessen the cost of keeping your house in working order. This chapter is filled with over 120 ideas for cutting costs on telephone service, heating, cooling, electricity, gas, water, television service, cleaning, decorating and fuel for your vehicle.

Lowering Utility Bills

Utility and service costs can take up a large portion of your monthly budget. The good news is that cutting these costs by a fraction can add up significantly over the course of a year.

Heating and Cooling

During the hottest summer days and the coldest winter nights, heating and air conditioning costs can leave your budget begging for relief. Here are a few tried and true tips that will cut heating and air conditioning costs throughout the year.

Set the thermostat at a frugal setting: By setting your thermostat at 66-68 degrees in the colder months and 78-80 degrees in the hotter months, you can easily cut heating and cooling costs. According to the Department of Energy's

"Automatic and Programmable Thermostats Fact Sheet," setting your thermostat back 10 degrees for eight hours (while you are sleeping, for instance) can save up to 10% off your annual heating bill. If you own a heat pump, though, setting the thermostat at a moderate temperature and keeping it there is usually most cost-efficient. If you adjust the temperature dramatically with a heat pump, the energy used by the auxiliary heat to reheat the house will negate the savings gained by cooling it down. Look in the owner's manual for your heat pump or consult your heating contractor to determine whether your specific heating system can recover from a lowered temperature without using the expensive auxiliary heat.

If you are too warm or too cold, adjust your own attire. Use cotton flannel sheets and an extra blanket in the winter and you won't even know that you've set the thermostat down 2 more degrees! Install ceiling fans for use in the hotter months to cool things down. Of course, the most frugal option of all is to turn off the air conditioner and heater and open your windows when the weather is temperate. Allow the fresh breezes to circulate through your home, saving you a bundle on heating and cooling bills.

Make your windows more energy-efficient: An inexpensive way to seal windows against the cold and heat is to install clear sheets of plastic specially designed for sealing. You can also add inexpensive window tint to cut down on the amount of heat coming through windows. A more expensive option is to add permanent storm windows with sliding glass and screens. Finally, you can replace your older windows with double-paned windows that have argon gas between the panes. The argon gas acts as an insulator because it is a poor conductor of heat. Visit your local home improvement center for more information on these energy-efficient ideas.

Improve insulation: Improve the insulation of the walls and floors that separate the inside of your house from attics, basements, crawl spaces and outside walls. There are many types of insulation, with varied R-Value (resistance to heat loss) ratings. Check with your local home improvement center for recommendations on how to better insulate your home.

Add weatherstripping: Weatherstripping is an easy and fairly simple way to reduce energy bills. Add weatherstripping to all your doors and windows. By preventing outside air from coming in through cracks and leaks you may be able to cut your heating and cooling bill by 20% or more. Also, use a draft stopper at the bottom of doors and seal any leaks around pipes under sinks.

Replace or clean your furnace filters every month: Keeping the furnace and air conditioner filters unclogged allows your heating and cooling system to operate more efficiently and last longer.

Use passive solar energy: In the winter, allow sun to heat your house by opening blinds and curtains and trimming trees that shade your windows. At night, close the blinds and curtains to keep the heat in. In the summer, keep shades and blinds closed to keep the warm sunlight out. Use awnings over windows to produce more shade. You should also plant trees to shade the air conditioning unit. A shaded air conditioner will use 10% less energy than one in direct sun.

Install an exhaust fan: Installing an attic exhaust fan in an attic window can significantly reduce the heat that builds up under your roof. A ridge vent also cuts energy costs by allowing heat to escape from the attic more easily. Speaking of exhaust fans, make sure you turn your bathroom exhaust fan on when you take a shower in the summer to reduce the humidity.

Cook for efficiency: In the hot summer months, avoid using the stove and oven. They release heat into the house and that drives up your cooling costs. Grill outside, cook in the crock-pot, toast in the toaster, or use the microwave to reduce the amount of heat being generated in your home.

Electricity and Gas
If your budget is in shock because of the high electric and gas bills at your house, it is time to make some changes. In addition to reducing your heating and cooling system usage, there are a number of easy and simple ways to cut back on your daily power consumption.

Turn off the lights when you leave a room: It's an obvious one, but turning off incandescent light bulbs when they are not needed can make a difference. A 100-watt light bulb costs an average of 20 cents per day. Over the course of a year, keeping a light on all the time can cost you $70. How many 60- to100-watt light bulbs do you have in your house? Because incandescent lights also generate heat, turning them off when not in use will help keep the house cool in the warmer months.

Install fluorescent light bulbs: Fluorescent light bulbs use about one fourth the energy of incandescent bulbs, but last significantly longer. They fit in the same sockets and produce the same amount of light. According to the Department of Energy ("When To Turn Lights and Computers Off To Save Energy and Money" Fact Sheet), it is probably most energy efficient to turn off a fluorescent light bulb if you are going to be out of a room for at least 15 minutes.

Use sunlight for indoor lighting: Open the shades to let natural light into your home and turn the lights off. This is especially frugal in the winter when the sunlight will help warm your home.

Find out if your local energy company has off-peak rates: Call your local energy provider and ask if they have off-peak rates. If they do, wash clothes and run the dishwasher during those hours.

Fill the fridge: Refrigerators and freezers are more efficient when they are full, so fill extra space with one-gallon drink containers. In a power outage, they will help keep things cool. Open and close the fridge quickly to reduce the amount of cool air that escapes. It takes a lot of energy to make up for the warm air introduced into the appliance each time you open the door.

Wash in cold and fill it up: Use warm, not hot, water for white clothes and only wash clothes (and dishes) in full loads.

Hang your clothes out to dry: Using the clothes dryer can cost more than 50 cents per hour. With 10 loads per week, that's $5 a week, or $260 per year. Keep the dryer lint free, which helps it run more efficiently, using less energy.

Use your small appliances: Use the grill, microwave, crockpot or toaster oven whenever possible. They use less energy than the stove or oven and your house will stay cooler in the summer.

Control the water heater: Changing the water temperature on your water heater from 140 degrees to 120 degrees can reduce your water heating cost by up to 10%, according to the Department of Energy ("Energy Efficient Water-Heating" Fact Sheet). Using an insulated water heater cover for electric water heaters can also reduce your water heater costs. Some newer water heaters are already quite energy-efficient and do not require a heater cover. Installing insulated covers is more difficult on gas and oil heaters. If your water heater is gas or oil powered, you should consult a local furnace installer for information and/or assistance.

You can put a timer on your electric water heater to control when it comes on and turns off. Usually the timer is set to turn off at night and resume heating in the morning. It is not as cost-efficient to use a timer on gas and oil water heaters.

Turn Off Your Computer: Save energy by turning off your computer if you are not going to be using it for two hours or more.

Water Use
Using less water really does save money. Here are some easy-to-implement ideas that you can start using right away.

◊ Switch from baths to showers. You can cut your water use for bathing by 2/3 by taking a shower vs. a bath!

◊ Take short showers.

◊ Install a low-flow showerhead to reduce the amount of water used by 50%.

◊ Don't leave the water running when you brush your teeth. Turn it on to wet your toothbrush, turn it off, and then on again when it's time to rinse.

◊ Wash only full loads in the dishwasher and washing machine. When you must wash a small load of clothes, change the water level to the appropriate setting.

◊ Use a front-loading washing machine instead of top-loading. The newer, energy-efficient models use less water and less energy.

◊ Scrape your dishes prior to loading them in the dishwasher. Rinsing is usually not necessary.

⚬ Fill a sink with water to rinse vegetables or clean dishes instead of letting the water flow continuously from the faucet.

⚬ When shaving with a manual razor, fill the sink with water instead of running the faucet to rinse your razor the entire time you are shaving.

⚬ Fix all leaky pipes or faucets as soon as you notice leaks.

⚬ Don't flush paper goods that could go into the garbage. Put them in the wastebasket to prevent using the water required to flush.

⚬ When waiting for hot water from the faucet, capture the colder water in a bowl and use it to water plants.

⚬ When washing the car, don't let the hose run continuously. Use a bucket of water to keep the car wet while soaping and turn the hose on for the final rinse.

⚬ Sweep your sidewalks clean instead of spraying them with water from a hose.

⚬ Use mulch in the garden and around plants to retain moisture.

⚬ Plant shrubs that are resistant to drought.

⚬ Water lawns and gardens in the evenings or early morning to prevent the water from evaporating before it reaches your thirsty plants.

⚬ Do not water your lawn more than is absolutely necessary.

TV, Cable and Satellite
This one is simple: canceling cable or satellite service will save you the most amount of money. If you want more channels than you can pick up using an antenna, consider basic cable for around $10 to $15 per month. Paying only for basic cable, without the premium channels, can save a few hundred dollars or more each year.

If you bundle services from the same cable company (purchasing cable TV service and high-speed cable internet service, for instance), you may also receive a better rate on the multiple services than if purchased separately.

Telephone Expenses

Cancel your landline phone service: Do you have a cell phone? If so, you may not need to continue spending the $30 or more per month that it costs to have a traditional telephone line (landline). Simply use your cell phone for all your calls. Make sure that you have enough minutes in your plan so you are not charged extra fees for using more minutes than you are allowed. It is usually less expensive to add minutes to your cell phone by changing plans than to keep your traditional landline with all the extra monthly fees.

Even if you don't want to cancel your landline, consider canceling your traditional long-distance telephone service. Many cell phone plans offer unlimited long-distance calling in the evenings and weekends. If your cell phone plan allows unlimited long-distance calls, or more long-distance minutes than you usually use with your landline, consider canceling your landline long-distance altogether. Use your cell phone for all your long-distance calls. We made this transition years ago and enjoy not having an extra long-distance bill every month!

Say goodbye to extra telephone services: Make sure you aren't paying for services you did not request or do not use. Examples include call waiting, voice mail and text messaging. Call the phone company as soon as possible if you see any charges on your bill for services you don't need or understand. Avoid using directory assistance unless it is an emergency. Save by using the phone book or the Internet to locate a number.

Calling cards: A great way to cut long-distance bills is to use a prepaid calling card instead of traditional long-distance from your landline. The 10 cents per minute rate you see with many long distance companies can't touch the low per minute rate you can get with a calling card. If you're paying more than 5 cents a minute to make long-distance calls, you're paying too much and need to consider other options. Even if you are paying 5 cents per minute with your long-distance phone carrier, consider the additional fees and taxes you are paying. With most calling cards, you avoid those extra charges. It is also handy to have a calling card available when staying at a hotel or in an area where your cell phone will not work. Check with your local warehouse clubs to find calling cards as low as 3.47 cents per minute!

E-mail and letters: One sure way to cut down on the phone bill is to e-mail more often. Although it's not the most personal way to communicate, you can e-mail at any time of day with no long-distance fees. The lost art of letter writing, although not as immediate as phone calls and e-mail, is still an excellent option for decreasing the phone bill.

Clean Up Time

We all know it is important to keep our homes clean and germ free. Dogs, cats, children, a messy spouse and basic daily living all add to the grime factor in homes everywhere. The key is to maintain cleanliness without paying full price for expensive name brand cleaning supplies. There are many ways to cut the cost of household cleaning products. If you prefer to use name brand cleaners, or you know you will not take the time to make your own supplies, wait for them to go on sale and then use a coupon to cut the cost by 50% or more. Often, using sales and coupons, I am able to purchase name brand cleaning products for less money than it would cost me to make my own cleaning mixtures!

If you are willing to make your cleaning supplies from readily available ingredients, you will spend less than the full cost of name brand supplies. Another benefit of using alternative cleaning supplies is that you will be exposed to fewer harsh chemicals, which your family and your house will appreciate. The top four cleaning agents that can handle most of your household cleaning needs include white vinegar, baking soda, bleach and ammonia.

An easy way to apply cleaning agents to most surfaces is by using spray bottles. Buy new spray bottles at a dollar-type store or hardware store. Label each bottle to avoid mixing substances that can be toxic when combined. Always use the same bottle for the same item. For instance, put your ammonia/water mixture in the same bottle each time. Use a different bottle for your bleach/water mixture. Following are tips for using these cleaning agents to keep your house sparkling clean.

SAFETY WARNING!
NEVER mix bleach and ammonia. Fumes created by this mixture can be deadly. Do not mix any products containing bleach with products containing ammonia.

White Vinegar
White vinegar is an excellent all-around household cleaner. It can be used as a stain and mildew remover, deodorizer, sanitizer, fabric softener, whitener, degreaser, polisher and more! The best part is that white vinegar is inexpensive and non-toxic so you don't even need to wear gloves. Vinegar does have a very distinctive smell, but the odor dissipates quickly and leaves a clean, streak-free surface.

Try some of the following tips and you will be surprised how effective and inexpensive vinegar can be when it comes to cleaning.

• Fill a spray bottle with full strength white vinegar for cleaning and deodorizing. Spray the soiled surface and wipe clean with a cloth or paper towel. Clean the bathtub, toilet, sink and countertops in your bathroom using white vinegar. Wipe down countertops, the refrigerator, doorknobs and the stovetop, as well. No rinsing is necessary.

• Clean windows by filling a spray bottle with 2 cups of water, ¼ cup white vinegar and ¼ teaspoon liquid dish soap. Spray on windows and wipe clean with a crumpled newspaper.

• Clean your microwave by placing 1 tablespoon vinegar, 1 drop of liquid dish soap and 1 cup of warm water in a small microwave bowl. Place the bowl in the microwave and heat on high for 3 minutes. Let stand in the microwave for 15 minutes. Remove the bowl and wipe the microwave clean with a damp cloth or sponge.

• Deodorize the kitchen drain by pouring a cup of white vinegar down the drain once every 7-10 days. Let it stand 30 minutes, then flush with cold water.

Baking Soda
Baking soda is a very effective and non-toxic all-purpose cleaner, deodorizer and stain remover.

Here are some practical uses for cleaning with baking soda:

• The most well known use of baking soda is as a deodorizer in the refrigerator. Place an open box on a back shelf in the refrigerator and replace every two months. Pour the old baking soda down the drain in the kitchen sink to deodorize the drain.

• Use 4 tablespoons of baking soda to 1 quart of water for an all-purpose cleaner. Use it to wipe countertops and remove stains and odors from plastic containers.

- Remove baked on food from pots and pans using baking soda. Sprinkle the burnt food with baking soda, pour in 2-3 cups of water, bring to a boil, remove from heat, let stand 30 minutes and the food should wipe right off the pan.

- Clean your refrigerator, microwave and other small appliances by mixing 2 tablespoons of baking soda with 1 quart of warm water. After cleaning with a sponge or cloth, wipe dry.

- Sprinkle baking soda onto carpets, wait 30 minutes and vacuum to deodorize. Test a spot on your carpet first, to make sure there is no staining.

- Remove odors in your laundry by using ¼ cup with each load in the rinse cycle.

- Deodorize a cat litter box by sprinkling a few tablespoons of baking soda in the bottom of the box before pouring in the litter. This is often less expensive than purchasing litter with a deodorizer already added.

- To unclog a slow running sink, pour baking soda down the drain followed by hot water.

- See http://www.armandhammer.com/ for many more uses for baking soda.

Bleach
Bleach is ideal for killing germs, whitening and removing mildew. This inexpensive cleaner is best used when diluted with water. Use the following tips to sanitize your household surfaces and keep germs away.

- Mix 1 teaspoon of bleach with one quart of water for general cleaning. Keep a spray bottle with this mixture for sanitizing cutting boards, sinks, kitchen and bathroom countertops.

- For tough stains and mildew, use a mixture of ½ bleach and ½ water in a spray bottle. This is an especially effective method for eliminating mold in a well-ventilated shower.

- To get rid of tea and coffee stains from mugs, let a cup sit overnight with the ½ bleach and ½ water mixture. Rinse and wash mug as usual in the morning.

- Do not let a bleach and water mixture come into contact with anything that can lose color, such as clothing or rugs.

- See http://www.clorox.com for other recommended cleaning solutions.

Ammonia
Ammonia is used effectively for cleaning many surfaces, including walls, windows, sinks, tile and floors.

NEVER mix ammonia with bleach.
The resulting fumes are toxic.

Place a couple drops of ammonia in a quart of water and spray on windows for a clear view. Use newspaper to wipe the windows dry and leave a streak-free shine.

Use ammonia to clean a greasy oven by placing ½ cup of full strength ammonia in a glass bowl. Leave the bowl in a cool oven overnight. In the morning, use a cloth dipped in hot, soapy water to wipe the oven clean. If there is any remaining baked on food on the oven walls, use a steel wool scrubber to remove the residue.

Use Less Paper
When cleaning the house, it may be easy to grab a handful of paper towels, but that convenience is costly. Save the paper towels and start using reusable cleaning tools. Your budget will thank you!

- Recycle old towels, socks and t-shirts to use as cleaning cloths around the house.

- Use crumpled newspaper to wipe windows clean after spraying. Your windows will have a wonderful shine with no residue or streaking!

- Revitalize your sponge by washing it on the top rack of the dishwasher.

- Use old toothbrushes for scrubbing grout, stains on clothing and hard to reach corners.

- Use cloth napkins instead of paper napkins when eating.

- Only use half a paper towel when you do use one.

- Teach your children how much toilet paper is appropriate to use.

- Dust with used dryer sheets. They do a wonderful job and cost far less than a disposable dust cloth. You can also dust with old socks by placing them over your hands. Kids love to help when they can use a dusting puppet!

For a wonderful Spring cleaning list that includes recipes for cleaning solutions, see All Things Frugal at: http://www.allthingsfrugal.com/sp_clean.htm.

See http://www.frugalfun.com/cleansers.html for even more frugal cleaning ideas and mixtures.

Decorating Deals

When decorating, you do not have to spend a lot of money to change the look of a room. If you take your time and do your homework, you can furnish and decorate a room frugally in the style you want. If you do not wish to spend your hard earned money on pricey home furnishings from the elite retailers, frugal decorating may be the answer for you!

What's Your Style?

When first planning to decorate a room, or even an entire house, get an idea of what styles you like. Look through any decorating and architecture magazines you can find. Ask friends if they subscribe to any magazines with decorating sections and ask to borrow them. Go to the library and home improvement stores and look through books and magazines to discover which styles appeal most to you. If you own the magazine, tear out the pages of decorating ideas and furniture that you like. Start a folder and keep it full of decorating styles that interest you. Use the ideas in the folder to inspire your decorating projects.

For some great decorating advice, tap into the expertise at home improvement and department stores. They often have professionals on site that can give you knowledgeable, free advice on floor layout and design, as well as decorating ideas.

Quick Fixes

There are a number of ways to change the look of a room quickly yet tastefully.

• One sure way to inexpensively and quickly add color to a room is to paint the walls. For great ideas on color schemes, visit your local home improvement store or paint store and look through the vast selection of decorating books. Many home improvement stores now have computerized programs in the paint department that allow you to create a room with any paint combinations you choose. This is a wonderful way to see how colors will look together. Home improvement and paint stores also sell paint mixing mistakes at a greatly reduced price. Often, these mistakes are merely the result of a mixing error that resulted in a color different from what a customer required.

- Use what you already have to change the look of a room. Items in the attic or spare bedroom may take on a whole new look in a different part of the house.

- Wallpaper is another classic way to add style to a room. To reduce cost, consider using wallpaper borders in conjunction with new paint. Most wallpaper stores also have a section of previously opened, discontinued or returned wallpaper. These rolls can be purchased at a fraction of the cost of special orders.

- Window treatments, such as curtains and valances, can be found at reasonable prices at yard sales and thrift stores. People redecorate and sell beautiful, well-made curtains for next to nothing. If you know of someone who is redecorating a room, ask if they will be selling the old window treatments. You may find a fabulous deal without having to look very far!

- Wait until the end of a season to purchase seasonal curtains and valances at deep discounts.

- Use mirrors to make a room appear larger and lighter.

- Plants immediately add beauty to a room with very little work. Some easy-growing indoor plants include Boston Fern, Grape Ivy, Philodendron, Spider Plant and Wandering Jew.

- Flowers from your garden, or a generous neighbor's garden, add color and a wonderful scent to any room.

Finding Great Buys on Home Furnishings

There are a number of places to find inexpensive home furnishings. When looking at used furniture, remember that mildewed upholstery is extremely difficult to clean, so avoid those pieces. Wicker furniture is very costly to repair, so think twice about those items, as well.

Yard Sales/Garage Sales: When buying furniture at yard sales, there are a few tips to remember.

- If you see a phone number listed with a garage sale advertised in the paper, call ahead and ask if they have the specific items you are seeking. Some sellers will let you have a "sneak peak" the evening before the sale and many will even allow you to buy at that time.

- If you do not own a truck or van, see if you can borrow one from a friend. Furniture is bulky and you want to be able to take it with you when you purchase it.

- The earlier you head out to the yard sales, the better the selection. Many garage sales start between 6:00 a.m. and 7:00 a.m., so be prepared to get an early start.

- Bring plenty of drinks and snacks so you do not stop at a convenience store along the way for high-priced refreshments.

- Take cash, since most yard sales will not accept credit cards or checks.

- Look for furniture items that can be refinished or recovered.

- Consider furniture for uses other than the obvious. For instance, if you need more shelving space in your laundry room for your overstock of canned goods, consider a sturdy used bookshelf. I have seen a number of these at yard sales for a fraction of the cost of shelving units available in home improvement stores.

- Don't be afraid to bargain with the seller. If you see an item you like but the price is higher than you want to spend, make an offer. If the offer is lower than the seller wants to accept, he or she may make a counter offer. Sometimes, sellers will go very low on the prices at the end of the yard sale. If you see an item but will not pay as much as the seller is asking at 7:00 am, come back at noon and make the offer again. If the item is still available, you may get a great deal!

- Moving sales are often great places to find quality items at bargain prices.

- Check newspapers for listings of yard sales in your area. Look for signs at subdivision entrances to find unadvertised yard sales.

Consignment Stores: Consignment stores often sell both new and used furniture and can offer some wonderful buys. I have seen new high quality name brand pieces at half the retail cost. Often these pieces are floor models with little to no wear.

Thrift Stores: There are some excellent buys to be found at thrift stores. If you look regularly, you may find just the piece you want at a very low cost. Sometimes you can find entire sets, such as a bedroom set or dining room set, for one quarter of the retail price. Thrift stores in more affluent communities will usually have a better selection of high quality furniture.

Flea Markets: Many of the same tips apply to both flea markets and yard sales. Arrive early, bargain, comparison shop, and make offers at the end of the day to get the lowest prices (as long as the item is still available). If a vendor does not carry the type of item you want, ask him or her to recommend another vendor.

Auctions: When bidding on items at auction, take advantage of the presale viewing. You will be allowed to look closely at the items and decide which pieces you find most appealing. Sometimes the auctioneer will give you an idea of how much he/she thinks the item will eventually sell for. Before bidding starts, decide how high you are willing to go and don't let yourself go higher. Don't get caught up in the thrill of the bid and then end up bringing home a terribly overpriced item. To find auctions in your area, check classified ads in the newspaper. You can also contact local movers for information about auctions for unclaimed goods.

Unfinished Furniture Stores: If you are willing to do some finishing work, you can find very good deals on unfinished furniture. We have three beautiful solid oak bookshelves in our home that we purchased at an unfinished furniture store for a fraction of the finished cost. My husband spent the weekend sanding and finishing the furniture and it looks professionally finished. Another benefit to finishing your own furniture is that you can choose exactly the color paint or stain you would like.

Showroom Samples: Throughout the year, furniture stores sell showroom furniture at healthy discounts. If there is a particular piece in which you are interested, ask the sales person if you can purchase the floor model at a discount. I have seen some floor models deeply discounted because of scratches that were hardly noticeable.

Freecycle: Freecycle is a grassroots organization with groups in many towns across the country. Each group is run by a volunteer who administers the local Web site. Freecycle allows members to offer and receive items for free. Many times, members are happy to give away perfectly good items to someone who will come pick them up. To find out more information, visit their Web site at http://www.freecycle.org and see if there is a Freecycle group near you. If not, consider starting a group in your community!

Friends and Relatives: When friends or relatives are remodeling, moving or downsizing, ask if they will be selling any furniture. Many times, relatives will simply give the items to you and friends will usually charge a reasonable price.

Newspaper Classifieds: Check the local newspaper classifieds for furniture.   Many people do not have time to sell their used items at yard sales and they advertise in the local paper or online classifieds.

When looking at used furniture, remember that many quality pieces can be refinished to look like new. With an electric sander and oil stain, you can make a scratched oak dresser look absolutely beautiful.

It is also important to consider quality when purchasing furniture. It is easy enough to find cheap-quality furniture at yard sales for next to nothing. It is worth the extra investment to buy a few pieces of high-quality furniture that will last for many decades and withstand daily use. Although we have a number of used, hand-me-down furniture items in our home, we have also invested in some solid wood, well-made pieces. These items will be in our family for decades and we will not be replacing them year after year because they fell apart. Keep in mind that we waited until we could pay for the furniture in full and we priced many pieces at different locations before making our buying decision.

Cutting Car Costs

The cost of owning and maintaining a vehicle can take up a large portion of your budget.   As gasoline prices have climbed to new highs and more and more people commute long distances, we are all looking for ways to cut the costs associated with driving. The good news is that there are ways to save on your transportation costs without resorting to standing on the side of the highway sticking your thumb out to oncoming traffic!

Improve Your Vehicle's Mileage
Following are some easy and effective steps you can take to reduce your vehicle's gasoline consumption, allowing you to get more miles per gallon.

- Follow the maintenance schedule recommended for your vehicle. Poorly operating spark plugs, dirty air filters and clogged fuel filters will all decrease mileage. The Department of Energy estimates that replacing a faulty oxygen sensor can increase efficiency by as much as 40%!

- Slow down. At speeds of 60 miles per hour (mph) or more, gas mileage decreases. For every 5 mph you drive over 60 mph, it's like paying an extra 15 cents per gallon.

- Fast starts and quick stops lower your mileage, sometimes as much as 30%! Don't put the pedal to the metal when starting, don't speed and don't slam on the brakes when stopping.

- Turn off the air conditioner, or at least use it less, when driving in the city or around town. When driving on the highway, roll up the windows to reduce the drag that decreases mileage.

- Lighten up your load by taking any unnecessary weight out of the vehicle.

- Keep your tires inflated correctly to improve efficiency.

- Don't use premium grade gasoline unless your car's manufacturer recommends it specifically. Check your owner's manual for recommendations.

- Fill your tank during the early morning or evening, when the air temperature is coolest. Gasoline is more dense during the cooler hours and gas pumps measure the volume of gas. You will get more for your money if you fill up during the cooler hours of the day.

- Use the highest gear possible when driving a manual-shift vehicle. Driving in a low gear may increase power and give you a fast start, but it also uses more fuel.

- Use your cruise control when driving on the highway and on flat surfaces. Hills cause the vehicle to speed up to maintain the set speed. The acceleration your vehicle performs on cruise control can be less efficient than manual acceleration.

- Avoid any excessive idling, including sitting in the drive-through line at a restaurant. When your car is idling you are getting zero miles to the gallon.

- Good aerodynamics increase fuel efficiency. Keep your car clean and don't carry bulky loads on the roof.

- Combine trips to reduce fuel use. When running errands, plan your route for greatest efficiency with the least amount of backtracking. Taking many short trips to the store with a cold engine can use twice as much gas as combining the errands into one trip, according to the Department of Energy.

- If your employer allows, telecommute. Working from home just one to two days a week will decrease your fuel consumption.

- Choose a fuel-efficient vehicle when buying a car. Take a look at the Consumer Reports annual car buying edition for information on recommended vehicles. Consider a gasoline-electric hybrid vehicle that gets excellent mileage.

Consider Alternative Transportation
There are a number of ways to get where you need to go without driving your own vehicle. Consider the following options to cut your fuel costs and decrease the wear and tear on your car.

Carpool: Carpooling involves two or more people sharing a ride. Carpooling helps reduce traffic congestion and pollution and is a strategy used by many people commuting to work. In some cases, those in the carpool share the driving. In other cases, one person does all the driving and the other riders pay the driver for gas and maintenance costs. Carpooling is not just for getting to and from work.

Consider ridesharing to get to school, sporting events, religious gatherings, entertainment venues and club meetings. To find a carpool group, simply ask friends, family and coworkers if anyone is interested in ridesharing or if they know of an existing carpool. You can start a carpool by asking coworkers who live near your area if they would be interested in cutting their commuting expenses in half or more, depending on how many people are in the carpool.

Vanpooling: A vanpool involves a group of employees sharing a van to ride to work. Passengers may be picked up at individual homes or at park and ride locations. There are usually one or two regular drivers who are not paid but get to ride for free. To find out about vanpool opportunities in your workplace or community, speak with Human Resources at your place of employment. You can also do an Internet search for vanpooling in your state. For example, type in "vanpooling, NC" to find out information about North Carolina state and local vanpool organizations. In North Carolina there is a free service called "Share the Ride NC" that offers ridesharing matching services all over the state. It also has information about park and ride locations, bicycle routes and public transit services. Many states offer this type of service and you should be able to find out more information by contacting your state's Department of Transportation.

Public Transportation: Most medium to large sized communities offer public transportation of some kind. Options may include buses, trains or subways. The cost of a bus or subway pass can be much lower than all the costs associated with driving, maintaining and parking a car in the city. Not everyone has access to convenient public transportation, but for many, this option saves them hundreds of dollars per year.

Biking and Walking: Biking or walking to get to work, school or the grocery store can cut costs and allow you to exercise each day. If you live close enough to your work, school, religious organization or shopping center, you can take advantage of the bicycle routes, walking paths and sidewalks that many communities offer. Even if your work or school is too far to commute by bike, use pedal power to run errands in and around your neighborhood.

Alternative Work Schedules

Many employers offer alternative work schedules, allowing employees to save time and money. Some examples of alternatives include telecommuting, working a compressed workweek (four 10-hour days instead of five 8-hour days), and working schedules that allow you to avoid heavy traffic times. Speak with your manager or human resources department to see if these options exist in your place of employment.

Key Points to Remember

- Costs associated with maintaining a household are a large part of most budgets. Apply the frugal living techniques in this chapter and your expenses will be lower, allowing for more aggressive debt reduction and savings.

- Compare the cost of national brand cleaning solutions purchased on sale with a coupon to the cost of homemade solutions.

- When making your own cleaning solutions, NEVER mix bleach and ammonia. The fumes can be toxic.

- Be creative when decorating on a budget. Use many different frugal resources to find a look that is just right for your tastes and your financial situation. Keep in mind that when you spend much less than full retail prices on decorating items (such as those treasures found at yard and clearance sales), you can make your home look like you spent much more than you really did. It'll be our little secret!

• Don't let your car and fuel costs drive you into debt. Improve your vehicle's mileage and consider alternative modes of transportation.

Key Actions To Take

• Set your thermostat to a frugal temperature right now. Better yet, shut it off and open your windows (if weather permits, of course).

• If you want to live a simple life, wish to cut some extra expenses or are living beyond your means, cancel the extra amenities that you do not need, such as cable, high speed internet service and call waiting.

• Buy spray bottles and suggested cleaning ingredients for homemade solutions and start cleaning frugally.

• Carpool to work or school just one day next week. You may enjoy the fuel savings and interesting conversation so much that you make carpooling a regular occurrence.

Chapter 7

Fun Freebies
and Extra Cash

Surveys for Pay

An easy and interesting way to earn a little extra money and receive free test products is to take Internet, phone and mail-in surveys. Surveys are usually administered by survey companies hired by manufacturers to find out how consumers feel about new products. The survey companies then provide the manufacturers with the resulting marketing information to help them determine what products they will introduce into the marketplace.

You may be asked your opinion about packaging, flavor options, product pricing, names for potential products and more. The survey companies usually contact you via e-mail or telephone to pre-qualify you for a survey. There are surveys available that pay as little as $1 and as much as $100 or more. For some surveys, the survey company will send full size products for a participant to test, including deodorant, air fresheners, shampoos, lotions or feminine products, among other things. Usually the companies that send free products to test also pay participants to give them feedback about the products. Some companies offer raffles as compensation and do not pay any money for survey completion, unless you win the drawing. Other companies send token gifts (such as pens, car shades) as appreciation for completing surveys. Each survey company offers different benefits for survey completion, so read the information about each survey carefully.

See http://www.freelancebyu.com for a long list of survey companies. From the home page, click on "Surveys 4 $" to view the many companies.

I highly recommend NFO (National Family Opinion) MySurvey at http://www.mysurvey.com. I have completed many surveys and free product trials for MySurvey over the last few years. They are professional, friendly, and easy to use and they have been in business since 1946. They reward you for surveys with points. After you reach 1000 points, you can cash them out for a $10 check or continue earning points for higher cash payments. Once you request a payout of your points, they send your check in a timely fashion. You can also donate your points to various charitable organizations or use points to buy raffle tickets for high value prizes.

There are many other surveys you can complete directly for manufacturers and service providers that pay money, offer a gift or offer a coupon. This is an easy and fun way to earn a few extra dollars with just a small time investment. It also gives you a sneak peak at the products soon to be introduced into the market by various companies. Visit http://www.phoenixfreebies.com and click on the section called "Test Products, Programs and Survey Sites" to find out about current manufacturer surveys.

Mystery Shopping

Mystery shopping, also known as secret shopping, is a fun way to receive free meals and earn money by evaluating businesses in your area. You probably won't pay your mortgage through mystery shopping earnings, but you may make enough to help with bills if you conduct many mystery shops per month.

Most mystery shopping companies have a similar process. First you register on their company website. Some companies contact you via e-mail or telephone when there is a mystery shopping assignment available in your area and some companies require that you check their website for available opportunities. Before you can complete a mystery shop, you have to read the requirements and qualify to be a mystery shopper for a specific store or business. While you conduct the mystery shop, you may be asked to purchase and return an item, eat a meal at a restaurant, place an order on the phone or other task. You will then evaluate the customer service, store cleanliness, wait time, stock availability, etc. Usually, you complete the follow-up evaluation form online within 24 hours after the mystery shop. You never let the store know you are conducting a mystery shop because it would influence the sales people if they knew you were "grading" them. See http://www.thefrugalshopper.com/articles/merits.html from The Frugal Shopper for some good information about mystery shopping.

Freelancebyu, at http://www.freelancebyu.com, has a number of links to many mystery shopping sites. When you go to the site, click on "Mystery Shops" on the left to view the information.

Freebies and Great Deal Alerts

Freebie sites are a quick way to fill up your mailbox with fun and useful trial size and full size products. Be careful, freebie hunting is addictive! You can receive many products just by entering minimal information on the Web sites of companies whose products you use everyday.

**Check out the following websites for
freebies and alerts on great deals:**

Freelancebyu: http://www.freelancebyu.com
Phoenix Freebies: http://www.phoenixfreebies.com
StartSampling: http://www.startsampling.com

Sign up for the Freelancebyu.com newsletter and every few days you will receive an e-mail with a list of fun freebies and good deals (also known as great deal alerts, or GDA's). These fantastic deals include online coupon codes and deals at brick and mortar stores.

Signing up for Manufacturer Giveaways is an easy way to receive full-size products just by making a phone call or by filling out an Internet form. Manufacturers offer giveaways for hand and body lotion, makeup, shampoo and conditioner, sunscreen, hats, toothpaste, candy bars, backpacks and many other items. Keep in mind that you won't win every giveaway since they are usually limited to the first 500 or 1000 people who enter. Find out about the dates and times for these product giveaways from the Freelancebyu and Phoenix Freebies Web sites. From the home page of www.phoenixfreebies.com, click on "Going Fast" to see the list of upcoming giveaways.

StartSampling, at http://www.startsampling.com, offers free full size products, trial samples of products and coupons. You can request one sample every 24 hours and the samples change from week to week. Manufacturers offer samples through StartSampling so they can introduce consumers to their products. The Web site also has a feedback section that allows you to let the company know your thoughts about a sample.

Key Points To Remember

- Learn about future products and earn a little extra cash by taking surveys on the Internet, by mail and by phone.

- Enjoy free meals, test products and earn extra money though mystery shopping.

- You can fill your mailbox with lots of fun and useful freebies just by filling out easy Internet forms.

Key Actions To Take

- Visit Freelancebyu and Phoenix Freebies for links to specific survey companies, mystery shopping companies, freebies and great deals.

- Register at StartSampling and choose the samples you would like to receive.

Chapter 8

Bank It, Share It, Keep It Up!

What To Do With Your Savings

Are you wondering what the best use of all your monetary savings could possibly be? The answer is: that depends. Where to put that extra money depends on your current financial situation and your goals for the future.

Pay Off Debt and Increase Savings

Whenever people ask me what my family does with the money we save using the techniques in the Smart Spending System, I give them the same answer every time. I tell them that we first paid off debt and now the majority of the savings goes into paying off the house and into our long-term savings funds.

 Although I am not a certified financial planner, I have read a tremendous amount of material written by the experts and my family has used that knowledge to develop financial goals and implement the processes required to reach those goals. We have worked toward a level of financial

discipline that constantly surprises and thrills me. Material wealth is not an important goal to our family, so our money goes to securing our short-term and long-term financial stability, not into purchasing lots of stuff. How you use your savings is up to you.

The key is to determine what is important to you and your family and set in motion the steps required to reach your goals. Although I have written this many times in this guide, I will stress once again that discipline is the key to financial freedom and peace of mind. If you keep the end goal in sight all of the time, you will be less tempted to use your savings for an expensive weekend in the mountains or on the newest flat screen TV.

If it helps, post your list of financial goals where you will see them everyday. Post them on the fridge, on the bathroom mirror or in your wallet. The constant reminders have helped many to focus on their long-term goals and sacrifice short-term pleasures to reach those goals.

Stewardship and Sharing the Wealth

There are wonderful and important things you can do with the freebies you don't need and some of the extra savings you realize from smart shopping. Are there any organizations to which you would like to donate more money? Would you like to be able to send a soldier a great care package that cost you almost nothing? How about putting together baskets of cosmetics, hair care, skincare and beauty items to donate to the local women's shelter or children's home? Isn't it nice to be able to bake a cake (for next to nothing using frugally purchased ingredients) for your neighbor who may be struggling with sick kids and a demanding work schedule? These are some of the ways we have given back to the local and national community in which we live. I am sure you can think of even more great ways to use your extras.

Schools

As any of you with children know, the schools are always looking for help in the form of money, time, box tops and donated items. Check to see what your children's school or the school nearest you needs and donate those items when you receive them as freebies or at a deep discount.

Lead by Example

As good stewards of your money, you will be able to teach your children and grandchildren the value of discipline and patience. As we know, children often model the behavior of the adults around them. Your financially responsible example is an important lesson they will remember their whole lives.

Keep It Up!

As you begin to use the techniques and methods in this book, keep in mind that nobody attempts the highest peaks when they are first learning to hike. It takes many shorter, less strenuous hikes to build endurance and increase skill level. All worthy endeavors take time, discipline and patience. Such is the case with frugal living, couponing and financial security. You will not become debt-free within minutes of completing your budget, nor will you have a frugally stocked pantry after just one shopping trip. It is important that you stay the course and use the techniques week after week to achieve the highest level of savings. As you make your way up the debt-free mountain striving to reach financial stability, remember that all the tools you have learned in this guide will help you make it to the summit. Keep your eyes on the goal and, once you reach the mountaintop, the view will be spectacular!

You have the ability to change your financial future and, once you decide to save more and spend wisely, you will feel tremendous peace of mind. As you go out into the world using the Smart Spending methods, continue to focus on your goals and on those things that are most important to you and your family. With each day, you will find yourself closer to financial freedom.

Enjoy your savings and always remember:

It's your money, spend it wisely!

Glossary

Term	Definition
B & M stores	Brick and mortar stores are those stores that are actual buildings at which you shop, not online retailers you only visit in cyberspace.
BOGO	Buy one get one free.
Budget	An itemized listing of estimated and intended expenditures and estimated income during a specified period of time.
CRT	Cash register tape.
Debt	Something owed, such as money, services or goods.
Debt-to-income ratio	Amount of debt owed in relation to total income. To determine your debt-to-income ratio, add your minimum monthly debt payments and divide the total by your net (after-tax) monthly income.
DND	Do Not Double. Found on coupons and indicates that the value of the coupon can not be doubled..
DND-9	Do Not Double, Triple, Quadruple, or multiply up to nine times.
GDA	Great deal alert.
FICO score	Developed by the Fair Issac Corporation, the FICO score indicates a person's credit risk. Scores range from 620 to 850. A higher score indicates a better credit risk.
Free Item Coupon	A coupon that allows you to get the product completely free. Often you will pay tax on an item even when using a Free Item Coupon.

FSI	Free Standing Inserts. These are the coupons inserted in the Sunday newspaper. Also referred to as SS (Sunday Supplement) coupons or insert coupons.
Loss Leaders	Loss leaders are the items that stores mark down significantly to entice you to shop in their stores. They may actually lose money on these items but they hope you will buy other items to make up for the loss leaders.
Manufacturer's Coupon	A manufacturer's coupon is a coupon issued by the maker of the product.
NED	No expiration date. Found on coupons and indicates that the coupon does not expire.
OAMC	Once-a-month cooking. Involves cooking and freezing approximately 30 days worth of meals during one weekend cooking session.
OAWC	Once-a-week cooking. One night per week, you make 7 batches of the same meal at once. You serve one batch and freeze the rest. In four weeks you will have almost a month's worth of meals in the freezer.
Price Book	A Price Book is a list of the items you use regularly and the best prices at which they sell.
POP	Proof of purchase. Usually is the UPC code on the package.
Store Coupon	A store coupon lists a store name and can only be redeemed at the specified store.
UPC	Universal Product Code. The standard bar code symbol for consumer product packaging in the United States.

Appendixes
Basic Budget Worksheet

Monthly Income		Monthly Expenses	
Your Net Monthly Wages	$	Mortgage or Rent	$
Spouse's Net Monthly Wages	$	Debt Payments (store and credit cards)	$
Part-Time or Seasonal Pay	$	Gas/Heating/Electric	$
Bonus Pay	$	Groceries and Non-Food Essentials	$
Tips	$	Dining Out/Take-Out	$
Commission	$	School Lunches	$
Investment Earnings	$	Water/Sewer/Garbage	$
Interest Earnings	$	Cable/Satellite TV	$
Rental Income	$	Home Telephone Service including Long-Distance	$
Social Security Income	$	Cell Phone(s)/Pager(s)	$
Pension Income	$	Home Repairs/Maintenance	$
Other Retirement Income	$	Car Payments	$
Alimony	$	Gasoline/Oil	$
Child Support	$	Auto Repairs/Maintenance/Fees	$
Unemployment Payment	$	Other Transportation (tolls, bus, train, subway fares)	$
Worker's Compensation	$	Child Care	$
Disability	$	Baby Sitter	$
Other Monthly Income	$	School Tuition/Activities	$
	$	Allowance	$

	$	Toiletries/Household Products	$
	$	Clothing	$
	$	Dry Cleaning/Laundry	$
	$	Uniforms	$
	$	Hair Cuts/Styling	$
	$	Gifts/Charitable Donations	$
	$	Religious Dues/Donations	$
	$	Home Owners/Renters Insurance	$
	$	Computer Expense	$
	$	Entertainment/ Recreation	$
	$	Hobbies/Lessons	$
	$	Healthcare (medical/dental/ vision, insurance)	$
	$	Life Insurance	$
	$	Interest Expense (credit cards, fees)	$
	$	Bank Fees/ATM Charges	$
	$	Savings Contribution	$
	$	Postage	$
	$	Magazines and Newspapers	$
	$	Personal Property Tax	$
	$	Pet Care	$
	$	Child Support/Alimony	$
	$	Service Contracts (pest control, lawn care)	
	$	Memberships (gym, clubs)	$
	$	Miscellaneous Expenses	$
Totals	$		$

Price Book Template

Product Type: _____

Date	Store	Item	Brand	Size	$	Unit Price

Smart Spending Resource Directory

BOOKS

Complete Cheapskate: How to Get Out of Debt, Stay Out, and Break Free from Money Worries Forever, Mary Hunt

Frozen Assets: How to Cook for a Day and Eat for a Month, Deborah Taylor-Hough

Frugal Living for Dummies, Deborah Taylor-Hough

Miserly Moms, Jonni McC oy

Not Just Beans, by Tawra Jean Kellam

Penny Pincher's Almanac, Reader's Digest, Edited by Don Earnest

Personal Finance for Dummies, Eric Tyson

So You Want to be a Stay at Home Mom, Cheryl Gochnauer

The 9 Steps to Financial Freedom, Suze Orman

The Complete Tightwad Gazette, Amy Dacyczyn

Your Money or Your Life, Joe Dominguez and Vicki Robin

INTERNET SITES FOR GENERAL INFORMATION

About.com
http://frugalliving.about.com
Contains information on all aspects of frugal living and saving money, creating a price book and frugal living.

Bankrate.com

http://www.bankrate.com

Excellent resource for financial information. Contains valuable financial calculators and articles.

Betterbudgeting.com

http://www.betterbudgeting.com

This site is full of information about budgeting, frugal living, frugal meals and living within your means. Sign up for the very informative newsletter and you will receive helpful tips and techniques through your e-mail every week.

Clark Howard.com

http://clarkhoward.com

Clark Howard is a nationally known radio personality who hosts a daily radio show. His Web site has a tremendous amount of information about saving money and making wise financial choices. There are also links to a number of other helpful sites.

Freelance BYU

http://www.freelancebyu.com

Anjie Hresan-Henley sends out an e-mail newsletter many times a week that absolutely spills over with great deals, including Internet clearance sales, coupon codes, B & M sales, freebies, contest information and more.

Organized Home.com

http://organizedhome.com

Wonderful resource for information about getting organized and freeze ahead cooking. Contains a number of useful templates including a price book page, pantry inventory, freezer inventory, menu planner and more.

Saving For College.com
http://www.savingforcollege.com
Joe Hurley offers excellent advice on saving money for college.

The Dollar Stretcher
http://www.stretcher.com
Created and edited by Gary Foreman, this Web site is full of useful cost-saving tips and advice. Sign up for the various newsletters and receive cost-saving ideas right in your inbox.

INTERNET SITE FOR ORDERING COUPONS

The Coupon Clippers (TCC)
http://www.thecouponclippers.com
Owned by Rachael Woodard, TCC is a professional and consistent resource for finding just the coupons you need.

INTERNET SITES FOR PRINTING COUPONS

Coupons.com
http://www.coupons.com
Print manufacturer's coupons from your printer.

SmartSource
http://www.smartsource.com
Print manufacturer's coupons from your printer.

FREEBIE AND GREAT DEAL SITES

Freelance BYU
http://www.freelancebyu.com
Find freebies, contests, surveys and great deals. Sign up for the e-mail newsletter for all the latest great deal alerts.

Phoenix Freebies
http://www.phoenixfreebies.com
Excellent website for finding freebies, contests, surveys and great deals.

Start Sampling
http://www.startsampling.com
Sign up for free samples of products offered by manufacturers.

MAGAZINES

Budget Living
Offers advice on living for less.

Real Simple
Offers information on living a simpler and more balanced life including recipes, natural remedies, decorating solutions, etc.

SAVINGS SITE

Upromise
http://www.Upromise.com
Sponsored by thousands of companies, this Web site lets you save money for college based on purchases of items you may already use.

About the Author

Faye Prosser owns Smart Spending and Couponing, a training and education company. Her mission is to help others become effective advocates for themselves and their hard-earned money. She teaches people how to budget, reduce debt, and save money on groceries and everyday purchases. Faye regularly conducts college courses and workshops at community colleges, parks and recreation departments, women's clubs and religious groups. She volunteers her smart spending skills to help various non-profit organizations, including Habitat for Humanity.

With the Smart Spending Grocery System, Faye's family saves over 50% off their weekly grocery bills and they are on track to pay off their mortgage before their children even start high school!

Faye's education and experience include a master's degree in Human Resources Development and over 15 years in management, training and consulting.

Faye, her husband and their children live in beautiful North Carolina with a dog, two cats and many fish.

Faye's motto when it comes to spending is:

"It's your money, spend it wisely!"

INDEX

A

ammonia, 124, 127
Annual Credit Report
  Request Service, 7-8
auctions
  coupons, 48
  furniture, 132-133
  gifts, 88
  restaurant certificates, 80

B

baking soda, 124, 125-126
birthdays, 80, 84-85, 86
bleach, 124, 126-127
BOGO, 35, 79, 151
breakfast
  breakfast for dinner, 68
  egg sandwich recipe, 73
  ideas for, 67
  freezing breakfast items, 72
  See also Food
budgeting
  Basic Budget Worksheet,
    153-154
  daily expenditure tracking,
    16-17, 18
  developing a budget, 14-16
  for gift-giving, 86
  for groceries, 62
  for holidays, 86
bulk cooking, 71-73

C

calendar of sales, 90
calling cards, 25, 123
car costs

alternative transportation,
    136-138, 139
  carpooling, 136-137
  improving mileage, 134-136
  vanpooling, 137
cash. *See* money
celebrations
  birthdays, 80, 84-85, 86
  children's parties, 84-85
  gift giving, 86-89
  holidays, 85-86
  parties, 83-85
cleaning
  ammonia, 127
  baking soda, 125-126
  bleach, 126-127
  spray bottles, 124
  white vinegar, 124-125
clothing
  coupon codes, 105-106
  department stores, 102
  discount clothing chains,
    102
  mass merchandisers, 102
  online coupons. 105-106
  online shopping, 104-106
  outlet stores, 102
  reductions on damaged,
    106
  thrift stores, 103
  warehouse clubs, 103
  yard sales, 103-104
  where to buy, 102-106
consumer debt. *See* debt
convenience stores, 21, 27
cooking
  bulk cooking, 71-73
  classes for fun, 92
  freeze-ahead cooking, 71-73
  once-a-month-cooking
    (OAMC), 71-72, 152